NO COMPROMISES

Encouragement
for the
Workplace

Rhonda Owen-Smith

BARBOUR
PUBLISHING, INC.
Uhrichsville, Ohio

NO
COMPROMISES

Published by Barbour Publishing, Inc.
P.O. Box 719
Uhrichsville, Ohio 44683
http://www.barbourbooks.com

 Member of the
Evangelical Christian
Publishers Association

Printed in the United States of America.

DEDICATION

First and foremost to Jesus Christ, my true Savior. To my husband, who has endured many lonely days and nights as God led me to put these thoughts in writing. He is a true inspiration and builder of my faith. To my mother, mother-in-law, and all the other "mothers" who care so much about me, pray for me, inspire me, and constantly remind me to take the time to care for myself while immersed in projects. To my deceased grandmother, Ethel Bell Taylor, who set an example of a truly God-fearing, faithful servant before I even had an idea of why she sat and rocked while she constantly read her Bible. To Reverend Tuggle for keeping me writing. To all of the people who said they thought this book would be a good idea, that they needed something like this, and "promised" to buy a copy. Finally, to all of the people I came in contact with during my corporate career, who kept me confused, challenged, disappointed, and distanced. There is a reason for everything; I just did not know at the time it was for this book. Thanks for the "inspiration" you gave me in your own special way not to compromise anything! May my love and God's salvation be with all of you today and always.

FOREWORD

The alarm clock rings; we rise and give thanks to God for allowing us to wake up another day. Then our prayers and thoughts turn to the workday ahead with its challenges. We pray for serenity and the ability to stay focused on God.

Every workday we are faced with demands, deadlines, decisions, and sometimes disappointments. Most days are made up of work we have to do, work we did not expect, things we simply do not want to do, and what we feel we do not have time to do. Then, there are the interruptions and unexpected occurrences that get in the way of accomplishing anything.

On top of that, we have the personalities to learn, accept, and work with—or work around. These personalities are those of our bosses, coworkers, suppliers, and others. The day has just begun and already things are not going as planned. Frustrations rise and tempers flare. People point fingers and they blame someone. Passing the buck is part of the game. People are whispering now in the bathrooms, mail room, hallway, and any other place where they can spread speculative gossip. The conversations are downright mean-spirited and vicious. Others look on, glad they did not get blamed this time. No one shows compassion for the faultless or an urge to correct the wrong.

Later, the rumors take on life and the wrongfully blamed cleans out his desk. Instead of sorrow or compassion, speculation begins with the question, Who will get the position? The jockeying begins, pitting so-called friends and colleagues against each other. Days pass by and people literally say and do anything to advance their careers. Finally, they fill the position. However, they passed over the person who is truly qualified for another. Again, another unfair decision. They shun the qualified candidate as if she did something wrong. She is depressed and discouraged; yet she must be quiet and go along with the program to keep her job. How unfortunate. The others do not care because they are glad they were not fired. Besides, they really do not want to work for a tyrant of a boss anyway. Just another day at work to think about and you haven't even left the house yet.

Before reacting to what has become typical in today's workplace, take a moment to reflect upon and apply God's Word, thinking about His perspective. Put Him before everything, no matter how small or seemingly meaningless. Acknowledge Him, and He will make the work, the relationships, the demands, the conflicts, and the temptations easier to handle—making the path He has for you clearer. Begin stepping over those stumbling blocks by viewing them as stepping-stones to God's kingdom. You may stumble, stub your toe, or skip a few steps. Yet view it all as a test and an opportunity to show your faith. There is a purpose for everything you witness and experience. Look for the opportunity to learn, lead, and teach. Most of all, have faith and know that God has expectations for you despite how things may seem. Don't question how or why; just ask what, listen, and then do. Let God guide your steps, thoughts, actions, tongue, and attitude. Walk carefully, yet upright and righteously, with full confidence that Christianity in the workplace is possible for you and for those you influence.

Personally, I have been there and made it through —both hindering and influencing others along the way. I have been on both sides of the desk, as boss and employee, and know firsthand the conflicts and compromises faced. I also recognize the undue challenges and demands I made on employees. I can see my failures and am glad that I am on the right track now. It took the Holy Spirit and many saints in the workplace to show me the right way to treat people, to handle situations, and how to influence others. Now, I hope something in this book can serve as your saint and help you deal with your coworkers, bosses, and employees. With a little conviction, I pray that you can tell others one day you have been there before—and made it through, too!

TABLE OF CONTENTS

ACCEPTANCE

Will they like me
    and respect my authority?
Or will I be talked about
    and shut out?
How are my clothes rated?
Are they outdated?
They call me the new kid on the block
    and they watch me around the clock.
Looking for some imperfection,
    ready to devour me as if I were a confection.
They view me through a magnifying glass
    as if it is their test I have to pass.
Through this inspection I stay focused on my
    selection,
looking only to God for my direction.

———————

Quick Script: John 15:18-19

If the world hates you, keep in mind that it
hated me first. If you belonged to the world, it
would love you as its own. As it is, you do not
belong to the world, but I have chosen you out
of the world.

UNACCEPTABLE
NONACCEPTANCE

Rejection hurts. We all know that. Sometimes we forget, though, that we are not only on rejection's receiving end; too often we are also guilty of not accepting others.

We like and dislike others because of things that mean absolutely nothing in God's eyes. Our opinions are based on trivial, exterior details rather than on people's interior hearts. We do not take the time to get to know each other, to know enough to even realistically determine if a person is someone with whom we want to associate.

Think about it—what do we really know about the man who sits in the office two doors down from our office? When we ask him in the morning how he's doing, do we stop to listen—or do we just keep walking, barely hearing or caring about what he said? Do we just speak because it is expected, having already decided not to get too close to this person?

Of course there are some reasons why we might not want to associate too closely with an individual. But then again, before we decide to avoid someone because of their "sinfulness," maybe we should ask God how He wants us to work in that person's life. We, too, are sinners, and we must leave the judgment of others to God.

We should be careful not to judge even the people who judge us unfairly. God did not say being a Christian was going to be the easiest thing, and it is particularly not easy in a workforce full of nonbelievers—or people who believe only part of the time, at their convenience. Are we currently ostracized or not accepted by our bosses or work peers? Well, then, we can remind ourselves that Christ understands; people rejected Him, too. But we shouldn't be so busy thinking about our own hurt feelings that we forget that Christians are just as fallible as others.

So, check your own thoughts and actions while you are busy checking those of your coworkers. We may never change the actions of others, but as Christians we can focus on how God sees us and how He wants us to see and treat others. Nonacceptance of others is unacceptable.

Top of Mind: Christ was and continues to be rejected by others. Strive for the worthiness of His acceptance, realizing that down through the years people have often judged His children unfairly. Being in the world, we also must be careful not to fall prey to the same judgmental trappings used against us. Reach out to all of your brothers and sisters in love.

Dear Heavenly Father, as I prepare for the work-day ahead, with all of its worldly challenges and opportunities to be a faithful servant, I pray to remain focused on You, Lord, remembering to grow in the glory of Your eyes only, as You are the One whom I want to please. Amen.

Words of Wisdom, Comfort, and Security

• It is okay be different. If you are a Christian, you will not be like the others.

• Christians have historically troubled those around them. Non-Christians will never understand why you do the things you do. Pray for those who persecute you because of your beliefs.

• There is no need to try to be popular and impress others. God has given you a special gift and He wants you to live up to the potential He has created for you—whether or not your achievement is ever recognized by others.

• If God accepts you, then whether others accept you really doesn't matter in the end. Whose acceptance matters more, your coworker's for today—or God's for eternity?

- Everyone is not going to love you or even like you, especially those who do not know God.

- Melt your enemies with your warmth. Almost everybody loves the people who love them back, but Christ calls you to love those who hate you as well as those who love you.

- The mark of a true Christian is being able to accept everyone—but it's okay to accept someone while not accepting their actions and attitudes.

- Do not seek the approval of others and lose favor with God in the process. Work toward God's acceptance and approval first, or you may work against His will.

- If you have to change, hide, or hold back anything about your Christian walk, then you are walking down a dangerous path.

- While you want others to accept you, are you accepting of them? Or are you more critical of those in the workplace than those at church? Are you more open to Christians than non-Christians? Check your acceptance level. Remember that God loves and accepts everyone.

Father God, thank You for accepting me as I am and allowing me the chance to learn Your desire for my Christian life. When others judge me, Lord, thank You for the comfort of knowing that You are the One whose judgment really counts and that You already showed Your love for me when You sent Your Son to die for me just as I was and as I am. Lord, since You have accepted me, I pray that You will help me to accept others without judgment. Amen.

SCRIPTURE REFERENCES

Matthew 5:10-12
Blessed are those who are persecuted because of righteousness, for theirs is the kingdom of heaven. Blessed are you when people insult you, persecute you and falsely say all kinds of evil against you because of me. Rejoice and be glad, because great is your reward in heaven, for in the same way they persecuted the prophets who were before you.

Matthew 5:43-48

You have heard that it was said, "Love your neighbor and hate your enemy." But I tell you: Love your enemies and pray for those who persecute you, that you may be sons of your Father in heaven. He causes his sun to rise on the evil and the good, and sends rain on the righteous and the unrighteous. If you love those who love you, what reward will you get? Are not even the tax collectors doing that? And if you greet only your brothers, what are you doing more than others? Do not even pagans do that? Be perfect, therefore, as your Heavenly Father is perfect.

Genesis 4:7

If you do what is right, will you not be accepted? But if you do not do what is right, sin is crouching at your door; it desires to have you, but you must master it.

Romans 11:15

For if their rejection is the reconciliation of the world, what will their acceptance be but life from the dead?

2 Corinthians 8:12

For if the willingness is there, the gift is acceptable according to what one has, not according to what he does not have.

1 Timothy 4:12-13

Don't let anyone look down on you because you are young, but set an example for the believers in speech, in life, in love, in faith and in purity. Until I come, devote yourself to . . . reading of Scripture, to preaching and to teaching.

John 15:18-19

If the world hates you, keep in mind that it hated me first. If you belonged to the world, it would love you as its own. As it is, you do not belong to the world, but I have chosen you out of the world.

Galatians 6:9

Let us not become weary in doing good, for at the proper time we will reap a harvest if we do not give up.

Hebrews 10:32-33

Remember those earlier days after you had received the light, when you stood your ground in a great contest in the face of suffering. Sometimes you were publicly exposed to insult and persecution; at other times you stood side by side with those who were so treated.

Hebrews 12:3

Consider him who endured such opposition from sinful men, so that you will not grow weary and lose heart.

1 John 3:13-14

Do not be surprised, my brothers, if the world hates you. We know that we have passed from death to life, because we love our brothers. Anyone who does not love remains in death.

John 5:41-44

I do not accept praise from men, but I know you. I know that you do not have the love of God in your hearts. I have come in my Father's name, and you do not accept me; but if someone else comes in his own name, you will accept him. How can you believe if you accept praise from one another, yet make no effort to obtain the praise that comes from the only God?

John 17:7-10

Now they know that everything you have given me comes from you. For I gave them the words you gave me and they accepted them. They knew with certainty that I came from you, and they believed that you sent me. I pray for them. I am praying for the world, but for those you have given me, for they are yours. All I have is yours, and all you have is mine. And glory has come to me through them.

Proverbs 21:2-3

All a man's ways seem right to him, but the Lord weighs the heart. To do what is right and just is more acceptable to the Lord than sacrifice.

Romans 15:5-7

May the God who gives endurance and encouragement give you a spirit of unity among yourselves as you follow Christ Jesus, so that with one heart and mouth you may glorify the God and Father of our Lord Jesus Christ. Accept one another, then, just as Christ accepted you, in order to bring praise to God.

BOSSES

Can't you see?
God works through you to direct and test me.
You may be gruff and unkind,
   but with God's help, in your heart something
   positive I can find.
Your demands may seem unfair,
   but for every task you ask, I can rely on God's
   care.
I will work as hard as I can to do the very best;
   if I did not, God would not let me rest.
I will treat you with respect and honor,
   just as I do my Father.
But, through it all,
I will remember that God is the only One on
   whom I call.

_____

Quick Script: Hebrews 13:17

Obey your leaders and submit to their authority. They must keep watch over you as men
who must give an account. Obey them so that
their work will be a joy, not a burden, for that
would be of no advantage to you.

TAKE TIME TO UNDERSTAND

As employees, our relationships with our supervisors don't have to be negative. Often, these relationships can be positive, learning experiences. Sometimes, though, our relationships with our bosses become fraught with tension. When that happens, we need to first of all examine our own hearts. Does the problem lie in ourselves? Are we having trouble submitting to authority? When the answer's yes, we need to reread Hebrews 13:17 and ask Christ to help us with our attitudes.

Sometimes, however, we are truly not to blame, and the problem lies with our boss's attitude instead of ours. Although there is no excuse for anyone to be treated improperly in the workplace (or outside the workplace), sometimes it helps to look beyond the situation and try to understand the person with whom we are dealing. Once we have an idea of the nature and character of our supervisor, God can help us deal with the person in a nonconfrontational, comfortable manner. Perhaps this person needs some specific prayer or even needs to accept Christ. We need to ask God for guidance.

Almost always, the first step will be for us to take the time to strengthen the relationship, letting the individual know that we value them. We must use patience and understanding, while overlooking and forgiving insults, slights, and offenses. Although it may seem difficult at times, God can use us to make a difference in this person's life. A solution-and-resolution approach to difficulties creates a respectful environment for working out differences. When we act with integrity, others will follow.

All people and situations are different. Not all bosses or relationships are bad, but God can make any relationship better. Pray for the best possible mutual relationship.

He Who Comes First: Let no person, object, or situation come before the One who was, is, and continues to be first. Keep your focus on the Creator, the Alpha and Omega of our lives.

Morning Prayer

Dear Father, as a child of Yours I pray You will help me be obedient to Your will. When my supervisors confront me with things that I am unsure of, let me turn to You always for advice and direction. Let me look to no other as my life's guide, either here on this earth or in heaven. Amen.

Statements of Fact and Faith

- Professional titles and positions of authority carry no heavenly weight.

- Do not take your lead from the "personalities" of the world or workplace.

- Prepare for the next action, day, and meeting according to God's direction. Don't go into work prepared with an armor of retaliatory assaults.

- Remember that your boss is human just like yourself and he will make mistakes. Give your boss the opportunity to learn from his mistakes.

- Do not persecute your boss by talking about her behind her back, influencing others against her. Remember, just as you do not want to be persecuted in your work, neither does she. Recognize the pressures that your boss may be facing on the job.

- Don't add to your boss's pressure. Instead be helpful and supportive. Have the same patience and understanding with him as you do with others.

- Give thanks for your supervisor. However it may seem, she was placed there for a reason. God can use what may seem like earth's worst for heaven's best, thereby increasing your faith.

- Seek peace and resolution with your boss. This is doing what God expects of you in any relationship. We must learn to give up and give in so we can keep our spiritual vows. Victory on these small earthly issues does not always mean eternal vindication.

- Focus more on what is right, not who is right.

- Often, the person who may be causing confusion and difficulty is really calling out for help. See how you can respond to this call.

- Respect your human boss, but revere your heavenly Boss.

Evening Prayer

Father God, I have completed my workday and I turn to You, Lord, for the leadership and direction I need to continue to serve You. I ask for daily guidance as I begin tomorrow and each day. Lord, help me to remain in Your favor and to influence those who are not. This I ask in Christ's holy name. Amen.

Scripture References

Romans 13:1-5

Everyone must submit himself to the governing authorities, for there is no authority except that which God has established. The authorities that exist have been established by God. Consequently, he who rebels against the authority is rebelling against what God has instituted, and those who do so will bring judgment on themselves. For rulers hold no terror for those who do right, but for those who do wrong. Do you want to be free from fear of the one in authority? Then do what is right and he will commend you. For he is God's servant to do you good. But if you do wrong, be afraid, for he does not bear the sword for nothing. He is God's servant, an agent of wrath to bring punishment on the wrongdoer. Therefore, it is necessary to submit to the authorities, not only because of possible punishment but also because of conscience.

Colossians 3:23-25

Whatever you do, work at it with all your heart, as working for the Lord, not for men, since you know that you will receive an inheritance from the Lord as a reward. It is the Lord Christ you are serving. Anyone who does wrong will be repaid for his wrong, and there is no favoritism.

Psalm 9:7-9

The Lord reigns forever; he has established his throne for judgment. He will judge the world in righteousness; he will govern the people with justice. The Lord is a refuge for the oppressed, a stronghold in times of trouble.

1 Peter 5:8-9

Be self-controlled and alert. Your enemy the devil prowls around like a roaring lion looking for someone to devour. Resist him, standing firm in the faith, because you know that your brothers throughout the world are undergoing the same kind of sufferings.

Luke 12:47-48

That servant who knows his master's will and does not get ready or does not do what his master wants will be beaten with many blows. But the one who does not know and does things deserving punishment will be beaten with few blows. From everyone who has been given much, much will be demanded; and from the one who has been entrusted with much, much more will be asked.

Luke 6:31

Do to others as you would have them do to you.

1 Timothy 3:1-4

Here is a trustworthy saying: If anyone sets his heart on being an overseer, he desires a noble task. Now the overseer must be above reproach, the husband of but one wife, temperate, self-controlled, respectable, hospitable, able to teach, not given to drunkenness, not violent but gentle, not quarrelsome, not a lover of money. He must manage his own family well and see that his children obey him with proper respect.

Ephesians 6:5-9

Slaves, obey your earthly masters with respect and fear, and with sincerity of heart, just as you would obey Christ. Obey them not only to win their favor when their eye is on you, but like slaves of Christ, doing the will of God from your heart. Serve wholeheartedly, as if you were serving the Lord, not men, because you know that the Lord will reward everyone for whatever good he does, whether he is slave or free.

Titus 3:1-2

Remind the people to be subject to rulers and authorities, to be obedient, to be ready to do whatever is good, to slander no one, to be peaceable and considerate, and to show true humility toward all men.

Ecclesiastes 8:5-8

Whoever obeys his command will come to no harm, and the wise heart will know the proper time and procedure. For there is a proper time and procedure for every matter, though a man's misery weighs heavily upon him. Since no man knows the future, who can tell him what is to come? No man has power over the wind to contain it; so no one has power over the day of his death.

CAREERS

Careers are like the shoes
　　we put on every day.
We try heels, loafers, and lace-ups,
　　trying to find the right fit in every way.
We look at titles, duties, and rewards
　　all to determine if the job is right.
But we often fail to realize that God
　　has a job for us, even if it's still out of sight.
We eventually fit comfortably in our position
　　and think we have it made.
Then those comfortable shoes begin to twist and
　　pinch.
While the pain becomes unbearable, we remember
　　how much we paid.
Maybe this is God's way of asking us,
Child, don't you think it's time for you to make a
　　change?
So we slip into another pair of career shoes,
　　even one that at first seems strange.
But by now we know not to question,
　　instead we just follow His direction.

———————————

Quick Script: 2 Peter 1:10-11

Therefore, my brothers, be all the more eager to make your calling and election sure. For if you do these things, you will never fall, and you will receive a rich welcome into the eternal kingdom of our Lord and Savior Jesus Christ.

WHAT DO YOU WANT TO BE WHEN YOU GROW UP?

So often we are asked this question, starting when we're still too young to know what it means to be a police officer, nurse, truck driver, or pilot. We blurt out an answer, only to change our minds in a week.

Many of us go through our working life still seeking the answer to this question. When we think we have found the answer, we accept a job—only to realize that it is not what we expected. Some of us go as far as attending college, getting a degree in a profession, only to work in the field for a year or two before deciding it is not what we want to do with our lives. We are not happy or satisfied.

The problem lies in that word "we." What's important is not what *we* want to do with our lives, but what God wants us to do. He has a plan for each of us.

Many ask, "How do you know when you are going against God's plan?" Simply, the sins of the world creep in and you will not be productive or happy. You may enjoy a short-term, false sense of happiness. However, eventually you will have no peace of mind or heart. You will not feel as if you have accomplished anything. You have no motivation or dedication. Things simply will not work out right no matter how hard you try.

If you find yourself wondering, "What am I supposed to do? What is my purpose in life?" turn to the Lord for the answers to your questions. These answers may come through gradual changes or opportunities, words of encouragement, something you read, or what someone asks you to do today. But most of all, God's plan for your life comes from His Word, your submission, trust, and obedience. Patience and trust are essential, because sometimes God may want you to do something that you have never done before, something that at first glance seems impossible. Remember, the God who created the world is big enough to handle your little life.

When you are moving in concert with what God wants you to do, you feel it in your heart, body, and soul. It radiates throughout for others to see. Your attitude and energy level are different. You feel a sense of purpose and can see the fruits of your labor no matter how big or small.

Don't let that burning desire in your heart go out. It was put there for a purpose. Step out on faith and see where God will lead.

Be All He Wants You to Be: Forget the career counselors. Patience and prayer presents God's predestined plan, especially designed for you. Don't shortchange your blessings!

Morning Prayer

Dear Heavenly Father, I offer a prayer to You this morning to ask for continued guidance and direction in my work. While I may be tempted to stray from Your plan for my life, I ask for conviction if I do, along with the brightest light possible to shine upon my path so that I can clearly see the way You want me to go. Thank You, Lord. Amen.

SOLACE IN SEEKING YOUR PLACE

•Your career is part of what God wants for you. God has a unique purpose for you that only you can fulfill. Without your part, the Kingdom of God would be incomplete.

- Allow God to work at His pace in your life. Let God plan your career if you really want fulfillment and "success."

- Who are you trying to please with your job or career? Christ? Or the world? Make it your ambition to be as much like Jesus as you can.

- How are you using your career or job to advance God's kingdom? Are you using your spiritual gifts and talents on the job—or just in church and around other believers?

- Do you take advantage of opportunities to gently witness to others at work?

- Be conscientious about your daily work, even those tasks that seem insignificant.

- When presented with a new job opportunity, consider if it will bring you closer or further from God. Will your career move force you to compromise any of your values?

- Put the same energy into finding God's will for your life as you do when planning your next career move. It pays to work and plan for an eternal future, rather than a temporary, short-term job.

- Your career is secure only through Jesus Christ.

Heavenly Father, I thank You for giving me the opportunity for another day to work out the plan You have for my life. Lord, I pray that my work today and tomorrow will be what You desire and that I remain open and trusting enough to take on any responsibility and opportunity that You present. In Jesus' name I pray. Amen.

SCRIPTURE REFERENCES

Ephesians 1:11-12
In him we were also chosen, having been predestined according to the plan of him who works out everything in conformity with the purpose of his will, in order that we, who were the first to hope in Christ, might be for the praise of his glory.

Ephesians 2:10
For we are God's workmanship, created in Christ Jesus to do good works, which God prepared in advance for us to do.

Romans 12:2

Do not conform any longer to the pattern of this world, but be transformed by the renewing of your mind. Then you will be able to test and approve what God's will is—his good, pleasing and perfect will.

Joshua 1:5

No one will be able to stand up against you all the days of your life. As I was with Moses, so I will be with you; I will never leave you nor forsake you.

Romans 8:28-30

And we know that in all things God works for the good of those who love him, who have been called according to his purpose. For those God foreknew he also predestined to be conformed to the likeness of his Son, that he might be the first-born among many brothers. And those he predestined, he also called; those he called, he also justified; those he justified, he also glorified.

Romans 12:6-8

We have different gifts, according to the grace given us. If a man's gift is prophesying, let him use it in proportion to his faith. If it is serving, let him serve; if it is teaching, let him teach; if it is encouraging, let him encourage; if it is contributing to the needs of others, let him contributing to the needs of others, let him give generously; if it is leadership, let him govern diligently; if it is showing mercy, let him do it cheerfully.

Ephesians 1:11

In him we were also chosen, having been predestined according to the plan of him who works out everything in conformity with the purpose of his will.

2 Peter 1:10-11

Therefore, my brothers, be all the more eager to make your calling and election sure. For if you do these things, you will never fall, and you will receive a rich welcome into the eternal kingdom of our Lord and Savior Jesus Christ.

2 Thessalonians 3:3-5

But the Lord is faithful, and he will strengthen and protect you from the evil one. We have confidence in the Lord that you are doing and will continue to do the things we command. May the Lord direct your hearts into God's love and Christ's perseverance.

Psalm 16:11

You have made known to me the path of life; you will fill me with joy in your presence, with eternal pleasures at your right hand.

Psalm 119:35-37

Direct me in the path of your commands, for there I find delight. Turn my heart toward your statutes and not toward selfish gain. Turn my eyes away from worthless things; preserve my life according to your word.

1 Corinthians 7:17

Nevertheless, each one should retain the place in life that the Lord assigned to him and to which God has called him. This is the rule I lay down in all the churches.

COWORKERS

Each of us is different,
 that's the way it's supposed to be,
  so how can I expect you to be like me?
Day by day and side by side,
 we sit together completing our task,
  so how's the other doing? Do you ask?
We need to take time to care,
 to break down those walls of jealousy and pride
  and share what's really going on inside.
As we share our concerns and cares,
 full of thoughts, ideas, emotions, and fright,
  we'll find ways in which we are alike.
Now we respect each other for who we are,
 knowing what to pray for and how to share.
Now we're part of the great story
 that tells of God's eternal glory.

———————

Now we ask you, brothers, to respect those who work hard among you, who are over you in the Lord and who admonish you. Hold them in the highest regard in love because of their work. Live in peace with each other. And we urge you, brothers, warn those who are idle, encourage the timid, help the weak, be patient with everyone. Make sure that nobody pays back wrong for wrong, but always try to be kind to each other and to everyone else.

CONFIDING AND CONFIDENCE

At work God calls us to make two commitments that have to do with human trust. First, He asks us to confide our feelings to someone else—and then He calls us to keep confidential what we've been told.

To confide in someone, we have to first have a relationship—and we can't have a relationship if we shy away from people, avoiding them because they're non-Christians. Of course, some people's beliefs and actions will hinder a close relationship—but we can't automatically deem everyone as untrustworthy. If we do that, we might as well not have the ability to write, talk, or communicate in any way. We would each be isolated from else, completely alone. But that's not the way God made us. He wants us to communicate, to reach out, to depend on others, and allow them to depend on us.

Although we can tell God everything, we still need to talk with another human being about work-related things. Sometimes no one else except a coworker can relate to our daily problems, because no one else we know works at a manufacturing plant, a shipyard, or a computer programming company. If we ask God for a confidant, in His time He will show us one.

The person to whom He leads us may at first seem like the most distant person at work, someone with whom we could never talk intimately. But when we make the first effort and then consistently keep reaching out to that person, we'll be amazed at what can happen. Even the person who at first seemed to be against us may end up as our greatest supporter. Remember, though, we can't ask for support without giving support. This is a reciprocal deal between ourselves and our confidant. We have to be committed to keeping confidential whatever our confidant says.

Sometimes, we may feel we have all the confidants at work we need. We may not be looking for a new confidant—but someone may be looking for us. That person may seek us out—or we may find ourselves being pulled like a magnet toward her. We may feel we just don't have the time or inclination for another friend, but when God presents us with the opportunity to show true love in this way, we shouldn't turn away with an excuse or we may miss an opportunity to be of service.

After all, we wouldn't want God to put us on hold

when we had a problem, would we? Whether we realize it or not, Christ may want to use us to be His lips and hands and eyes for this lonely person. Instead of being annoyed by this new demand on our time, we should consider it as recognition from God that He has faith in us and that His light will shine through us if we are only open and obedient to Him.

God has given His children the spirit of love and compassion. The world is full of the devil's toys: hate, lying, distrust, unfairness, prejudice, envy, gossip, and more—but Christ has overcome the world for us. Secure in His love, we can share with others and let them share with us in confidence.

Tempted to Tell: We know that the Lord answers our prayers according to His time and in His way. Many of us, however, still want an immediate response or solution—so we turn to another friend after someone else has revealed to us their personal issues. Human nature tempts us to tell what that person said, forgetting the hurt and damage that can come when secrets are told. The devil delights in confusion—we can't let our tongue get caught in this trap. Sometimes keeping our mouths closed is a hard discipline to practice, but Jesus wants us to keep others' confidences to ourselves. If we have to tell someone, we can tell it to God when we pray.

Lord Jesus, I thank You this morning for the job You've given me and for all the ways You have blessed me. As I work today, Lord, guide me in my dealings with my coworkers. Show me an opportunity to be of assistance and give me the strength to see adversity for what it really is—a spiritual challenge. Lord, stand with me in the battle to be trusting and trustworthy. Amen.

———

Working Together Requires Work

- You have the work God intended for you, not for your coworker. Get your own work done.

- With God in your heart you can love anyone, even those who do not love you.
- Don't compromise yourself and your relationship with God by trying to be like your coworkers.

- Don't let the actions of your coworkers create in you a spirit of ungodliness.

- Reach out to your coworkers instead of trying to turn and run away. Let God be the judge of what they do; focus on how you may help instead.

- Can you accomplish your job without the help of others? Can others accomplish their jobs without your help? Everyone has a job to do, and in God's eyes, no one's job is more important than the other's.

- Your coworkers are your brothers and sisters. Help them and love them just as though you were members of a family. Love your coworkers as you love yourself. God commands you to do so.

- You spend more hours a week with your coworkers than with anyone else in your life. Find a way to make the best use of the time together.

- You'll find some of the best role models and friends at work if you only look.

- Look for opportunities to bring your unsaved coworkers to Christ.

- Remember that we are all human and have our faults.

- Don't get so busy with your work that you cut yourself and your spiritual gifts off from those around you.

- Not everyone will be accepting of you—but God will always be.

- Demonstrate in the workplace the same compassion God shows you.

Heavenly Father, I give all honor and praise to You as I uplift Your name. I am grateful to have had an opportunity to do Your work while I work. I pray that through my actions, Your light has shined through me to that one person who needed to see it most. Continue to show me how I can help others, one by one. Amen.

SCRIPTURE REFERENCES

Colossians 4:5-6
Be wise in the way you act toward outsiders; make the most of every opportunity. Let your conversation be always full of grace, seasoned with salt, so that you may know how to answer everyone.

Romans 12:10-13
Be devoted to one another in brotherly love. Honor one another above yourselves. Never be lacking in zeal, but keep your spiritual fervor, serving the Lord. Be joyful in hope, patient in affliction, faithful in prayer. Share with God's people who are in need. Practice hospitality.

1 John 3:7-8

Dear children, do not let anyone lead you astray. He who does what is right is righteous, just as he [Christ] is righteous. He who does what is sinful is of the devil, because the devil has been sinning from the beginning. The reason the Son of God appeared was to destroy the devil's work.

Proverbs 22:24-25

Do not make friends with a hot-tempered man, do not associate with one easily angered, or you may learn his ways and get yourself ensnared.

2 Corinthians 6:14-15

Do not be yoked together with unbelievers. For what do righteousness and wickedness have in common? Or what fellowship can light have with darkness? What harmony is there between Christ and Belial? What does a believer have in common with an unbeliever?

Proverbs 22:29

Do you see a man skilled in his work? He will serve before kings; he will not serve before obscure men.

Colossians 3:23-24

Whatever you do, work at it with all your heart, as working for the Lord, not for men, since you know that you will receive an inheritance from the Lord as a reward. It is the Lord Christ you are serving.

Romans 12:16
Live in harmony with one another. Do not be proud, but be willing to associate with people of low position. Do not be conceited.

Philippians 1:27-30
Whatever happens, conduct yourselves in a manner worthy of the gospel of Christ. Then, whether I come and see you or only hear about you in my absence, I will know that you stand firm in one spirit, contending as one man for the faith of the gospel without being frightened in any way by those who oppose you. This is a sign to them that they will be destroyed, but that you will be saved—and that by God. For it has been granted to you on behalf of Christ not only to believe on him, but also to suffer for him, since you are going through the same struggle you saw I had, and now hear that I still have.

Philippians 2:14-15
Do everything without complaining or arguing, so that you may become blameless and pure, children of God without fault in a crooked and depraved generation, in which you shine like stars in the universe.

Galatians 6:1-5

Brothers, if someone is caught in a sin, you who are spiritual should restore him gently. But watch yourself, or you also may be tempted. Carry each other's burdens, and in this way you will fulfill the law of Christ. If anyone thinks he is something when he is nothing, he deceives himself. Each one should test his own actions. Then he can take pride in himself, without comparing himself to somebody else, for each one should carry his own load.

Galatians 5:13-15

You, my brothers, were called to be free. But do not use your freedom to indulge the sinful nature; rather, serve one another in love. The entire law is summed up in a single command: "Love your neighbor as yourself." If you keep on biting and devouring each other, watch out or you will be destroyed by each other.

Colossians 1:29

To this end I labor, struggling with all his energy, which so powerfully works in me.

1 Corinthians 3:8-9

The man who plants and the man who waters have one purpose, and each will be rewarded according to his own labor. For we are God's fellow workers; you are God's field, God's building.

CRITICISM AND JUDGMENT

With every word spoken
   and every thought imagined,
      hearts and spirits are broken.
An unblinking stare
   and a raised eyebrow
      burns through the heart, whether justified
      or unfair.
Reports at the end of the year
   just two pages long
      sting eyes, forcing a tear.
Jokes and poking fun
   can open wounds as if from a gun.
Through it all, remember the Son
   and all that He has done,
      for God is the true judging One.
Don't take the blame or feel ashamed.
   When those times come,
      remember to call upon His name.

Quick Script: James 5:9

Don't grumble against each other, brothers, or you will be judged. The Judge is standing at the door!

CRITICISM IS A GROWTH CHALLENGE

A critic's ultimate victim is himself. He robs himself of seeing the wonders of God in each person, situation, and environment. Like a thief in the night, criticism can steal self-esteem, happiness, motivation, and confidence. Criticism and judgment is a double-edged sword that swings toward the unsuspecting, often innocent, person and then returns like a boomerang to the critic.

As Christians, we are human and we can't help but feel a sense of hurt and disappointment when criticism and judgment are lodged against us. However, we have Someone to turn to for comfort. Christ's death has made us guiltless in God's sight, and His perspective is the only one that's true.

More important than our hurt feelings, though, is our responsibility to help the critic. Yes, help the person who complains all the time. As we look closer, we often see a person who is unhappy, insecure, and in search of attention. We may find a person who does not know God or has not grown in her understanding of the love and security He gives to His followers. It would be a shame if we focused on the criticism instead of on the needs of the person who is saying these negative things and thereby missed a chance to work for Christ's Kingdom. Meet the challenge head on!

Helping the Faultfinders: They judge and criticize, not always even realizing the hurt they have done; apparently they don't know the Son. They hurt inside, so they lash out, striking anyone and anything in their way. If you know someone like this, talk to them and pray for them. Do what you can to shine Christ's love and light into their misery.

Morning Prayer

Father, as I begin this day, I pray that you'll remind me not to criticize anyone. Guard me against conversations that are critical in nature. Lord, when criticism is directed at me, give me the wisdom to see it as a learning experience, knowing that I grow with every challenge to my Christianity. Thank You, Lord, for listening to my prayers. Amen.

TUNE OUT THE NEGATIVE
AND TURN UP CHRIST

- God's view, opinion, and verdict are the only ones that count.

- What God knows about us is more important than what someone says or thinks.

- If you look for something wrong, that is what you will find.

- Criticism chokes Christ and His joy out of our lives and the lives of others.

- God accepts us as we are, so there is no reason to be concerned with criticism by anyone other than Him.

- Christianity does not make us superior to anyone.

- Criticism comes from a hardened and hurt heart, helpfulness comes from a soft and loving heart. What type of heart do you have today?

- Was what you said a criticism, opinion, or an effort to help? Weigh what you say and do.

- If you listen to negative comments all day without saying anything positive, it is just as if you said those same harsh things yourself. Speak up for Christ. Consciously counter negative comments with positive ones and watch others catch on to positive communications.

• Remember that Jesus was criticized—and He lived a perfect life!

• No one is above constructive direction, including you. Look for God at work, think about what was said, then examine yourself.

• If we want to pass judgment, we need to start and end with ourselves. Don't forget that you must also give an account of yourself.

• Help others accept Christ; don't publicly criticize the devil-driven actions of those who don't know any better. Pray for them.

• Stop trying to do God's job.

———————

Heavenly Father, help me to always look for the positive, share a good word, and uplift others. I seek to honor You with my thoughts, actions, and words. Most honorable Father, thank You for allowing me to return honor to You by seeing others with the eyes of Christ—with love and acceptance. Amen.

SCRIPTURE REFERENCES

Matthew 5:11-12

Blessed are you when people insult you, persecute you and falsely say all kinds of evil against you because of me. Rejoice and be glad, because great is your reward in heaven, for in the same way they persecuted the prophets who were before you.

James 4:11-12

Brothers, do not slander one another. Anyone who speaks against his brother or judges him speaks against the law and judges it. When you judge the law, you are not keeping it, but sitting in judgment on it. There is only one Lawgiver and Judge, the one who is able to save and destroy. But you—who are you to judge your neighbor?

Psalm 109:26-31

Help me, O Lord my God; save me in accordance with your love. Let them know that it is your hand, that you, O Lord, have done it. They may curse, but you will bless; when they attack they will be put to shame, but your servant will rejoice. My accusers will be clothed with disgrace and wrapped in shame as in a cloak. With my mouth I will greatly extol the Lord; in the great throng I will praise him. For he stands at the right hand of the needy one, to save his life from those who condemn him.

Psalm 119:23-24

Though rulers sit together and slander me, your servant will meditate on your decrees. Your statutes are my delight; they are my counselors.

Romans 2:1-4

You, therefore, have no excuse, you who pass judgment on someone else, for at whatever point you judge the other, you are condemning yourself, because you who pass judgment do the same things. Now we know that God's judgment against those who do such things is based on truth. So when you, a mere man, pass judgment on them and yet do the same things, do you think you will escape God's judgment? Or do you show contempt for the riches of his kindness, tolerance and patience, not realizing that God's kindness leads you towards repentance?

Matthew 7:1-5

Do not judge, or you too will be judged. For in the same way you judge others, you will be judged, and with the measure you use, it will be measured to you. Why do you look at the speck of sawdust in your brother's eye and pay no attention to the plank in your own eye? How can you say to your brother, "Let me take the speck out of your eye," when all the time there is a plank in your own eye? You hypocrite, first take the plank out of your own eye, and then you will see clearly to remove the speck from your brother's eye.

Psalm 120:1-4

I call on the Lord in my distress, and he answers me. Save me, O Lord, from lying lips and from deceitful tongues. What will he do to you, and what more besides, O deceitful tongue? He will punish you with a warrior's sharp arrows, with burning coals of the broom tree.

Lamentations 3:58-62

O Lord, you took up my case; you redeemed my life. You have seen, O Lord, the wrong done to me. Uphold my cause! You have seen the depth of their vengeance, all their plots against me. O Lord, you have heard their insults, all their plots against me—what my enemies whisper and mutter against me all day long.

Proverbs 24:17-21

Do not gloat when your enemy falls; when he stumbles, do not let your heart rejoice, or the Lord will see and disapprove and turn his wrath away from him. Do not fret because of evil men or be envious of the wicked, for the evil man has no future hope, and the lamp of the wicked will be snuffed out. Fear the Lord and the king, my son, and do not join with the rebellious.

Isaiah 41:9-13

I took you from the ends of the earth, from its farthest corners I called you. I said, 'You are my servant'; I have chosen you and have not rejected you. So do not fear, for I am with you; do not be dismayed, for I am your God. I will strengthen you and help you; I will uphold you with my righteous right hand. All who rage against you will surely be ashamed and disgraced; those who oppose you will be as nothing and perish. Though you search for your enemies, you will not find them. Those who wage war against you will be as nothing at all. For I am the Lord, your God, who takes hold of your right hand and says to you, Do not fear; I will help you.

Romans 14:10-13

You, then, why do you judge your brother? Or why do you look down on your brother? For we will all stand before God's judgment seat. It is written: "'As surely as I live,' says the Lord, 'every knee will bow before me; every tongue will confess to God.'" So then, each of us will give an account of himself to God. Therefore, let us stop passing judgment on one another. Instead, make up your mind not to put any stumbling block or obstacle in your brother's way.

Psalm 106:3-5

Blessed are they who maintain justice, who constantly do what is right. Remember me, O Lord, when you show favor to your people, come to my aid when you save them, that I may enjoy the prosperity of your chosen ones, that I may share in the joy of your nation and join your inheritance in giving praise.

DEPRESSION

Depression is the devil's discouragement.
Discouragement is how the devil creates doubt.
Doubt is confusion the devil controls.
Control is the devil's desire to rule.
Rule is responding to the devil's command.
Command is the devil's demand.
Demand is the devil's desire.
Desire is the devil's enticement.
Enticement is the devil's lure.
Lure is the devil's lustful bait.
Bait is the devil's convincing, deep hook.
Hook is the piercing force of the devil's bondage.
Bondage is the devil's evil hold.
Hold is the devil's wish.
Wish is the devil's plan to end eternal life.
Eternal life is what the devil wants to take.
Take hold, or the devil will dismiss this
    reminder of what you stand to risk
        if you turn away from Christ's saving power.

"My grace is sufficient for you, for my power is made perfect in weakness." Therefore I will boast all the more gladly about my weaknesses, so that Christ's power may rest on me. That is why, for Christ's sake, I delight in weaknesses, in insults, in persecutions, in difficulties. For when I am weak, then I am strong.

"Don't Worry, Be Happy"

"Don't Worry, Be Happy" is the title of a popular song that hit the charts several years ago. People wore T-shirts with the title imprinted on the fronts, used the title in conversations, and even went so far as to put it on their answering machines. The use of this song title is practically gone now, just like other fads. However, for Christians there is a message of faith in the title that should never go away. In fact, it should grow stronger and become an even larger part of our lives as we face faith challenges, growing spiritually.

When you feel alone with nowhere to turn—don't worry, be happy. Leave behind what happened in the past. Don't be burdened by the events of the day. Nor should you be concerned about the next day. Don't worry, be happy. Be happy that when you accepted Christ, He gave you a new lease on life, one full of peace. Liberate your mind from whatever the devil is using as a depressant. Concentrate on how God sets your soul free, uplifts you, and gives you inner peace.

When you see others downcast and downtrodden, remind them: don't worry and be happy about all that the Lord has done. The best is yet to come.

———————

Dismissing Depression: When you accepted Christ, you received the blessing of eternal life and a peace so wonderful that you can't possibly find enough words to describe it. You also were given the ability to see God at work around. Don't let worldly conditions deaden, disrupt, and destroy your destiny. The devil uses depression as a divide-and-conquer technique, separating you from your relationship with God and the power of prayer.

———————

Most honorable Father, prayerfully I ask for a spirit of mindfulness today of all that You have done for me. Regardless of what I face today, Lord, I pray that I will keep my eyes, mind, and spirit uplifted and focused on Your goodness. Lord, thank You for keeping me looking up. Amen.

REMAIN ENCOURAGED BY TAKING THE "DIS" OUT OF DISCOURAGE

- Seek comfort with God. Let Him handle your battles, troubles, and conflicts. Remember that in the midst of life's problems, He never forsook Paul and David, Peter and Abraham, Stephen and Moses. He will be just as faithful in your own life.

- You may think you have tried your hardest, but until you call upon God, your burden will remain. Stop struggling with things that only the strength of God can overcome.

- With every challenge, you have the opportunity to experience greater growth in your faith and your walk with God. God uses the most painful trials to keep you reliant and faithful. His love does not keep you from challenges, but sees you through them clearly.

•Perhaps one of the reasons you have depression and discouragement is because you have not yielded everything totally to God.

•Don't let problems get you down—let them remind you to look up. Count your blessings, see the ones around you now, and get excited about those that are to come. Tune into God and change the channel away from your depressed thoughts.

•Nothing can hold the Holy Spirit down—everything lifts Him up.

•There is no problem too big for God to handle, but He can't help if you don't hand it over to Him.

———————

Honorable Father in heaven, please help me to remember all the good that You have done for me and all that You promise for the future. Let me not forget that You are always with me and that I can always turn to You. Lord, help me realize that the devil is the oppressor and depressor and to always ask for deliverance. Amen.

SCRIPTURE REFERENCES

Psalm 42:11
Why are you downcast, O my soul? Why so disturbed within me? Put your hope in God, for I will yet praise him, my Savior and my God.

Ecclesiastes 7:3
Sorrow is better than laughter, because a sad face is good for the heart.

Psalm 55:22
Cast your cares on the Lord and he will sustain you; he will never let the righteous fall.

Psalm 62:5-8

Find rest, O my soul, in God alone; my hope comes from him. He alone is my rock and my salvation; he is my fortress, I will not be shaken. My salvation and my honor depend on God; he is my mighty rock, my refuge. Trust in him at all times, O people; pour out your hearts to him, for God is our refuge.

Psalm 30:10-12

"Hear, O Lord, and be merciful to me; O Lord, be my help." You turned my wailing into dancing; you removed my sackcloth and clothed me with joy, that my heart may sing to you and not be silent. O Lord my God, I will give you thanks forever.

1 Thessalonians 5:9-11

For God did not appoint us to suffer wrath but to receive salvation through our Lord Jesus Christ. He died for us so that, whether we are awake or asleep, we may live together with him. Therefore, encourage one another and build each other up, just as in fact you are doing.

Isaiah 43:2

When you pass through the waters, I will be with you; and when you pass through the rivers, they will not sweep over you. When you walk through the fire, you will not be burned; the flames will not set you ablaze.

Job 4:2-7

If someone ventures a word with you, will you be impatient? But who can keep from speaking? Think how you have instructed many, how you have strengthened feeble hands. Your words have supported those who stumbled; you have strengthened faltering knees. But now trouble comes to you, and you are discouraged; it strikes you, and you are dismayed. Should not your piety be your confidence and your blameless ways your hope? Consider now: Who, being innocent, has ever perished? Where were the upright ever destroyed?

Ecclesiastes 7:13-14

Consider what God has done: Who can straighten what he has made crooked? When times are good, be happy; but when times are bad, consider: God has made the one as well as the other. Therefore, a man cannot discover anything about his future.

Isaiah 50:10

Who among you fears the Lord and obeys the word of his servant? Let him who walks in the dark, who has no light, trust in the name of the Lord and rely on his God.

Psalm 107:28-32

Then they cried out to the Lord in their trouble, and he brought them out of their distress.

He stilled the storm to a whisper; the waves of the sea were hushed. They were glad when it grew calm, and he guided them to their desired haven. Let them give thanks to the Lord for his unfailing love and his wonderful deeds for men. Let them exalt him in the assembly of the people and praise him in the council of the elders.

2 Corinthians 1:3-7

Praise be to the God and Father of our Lord Jesus Christ, the Father of compassion and the God of all comfort, who comforts us in all our troubles, so that we can comfort those in any trouble with the comfort we ourselves have received from God. For just as the sufferings of Christ flow over into our lives, so also through Christ our comfort overflows. If we are distressed, it is for your comfort and salvation; if we are comforted, it is for your comfort, which produces in you patient endurance of the same sufferings we suffer. And our hope for you is firm, because we know that just as you share in our sufferings, so also you share in our comfort.

DISCRIMINATION

Discrimination can be anywhere.
   Those who practice it don't care.
Subtle or blatant it does exist.
   It's something we all must resist.
Maybe we blame our parents for its instilling,
   but letting it take root in our heart is killing.
It takes our spiritual life away,
   and hurts innocent people for day after day.
The names called as children or unfairness shown,
   remains as a memory until the child is grown.
This must end whether it has been committed by
      others,
   or if we too practice this sin against our
      brothers.
We must ask for forgiveness and forgive,
   that's what God expects while on earth we live.

Quick Script: Romans 15:7

Accept one another, then, just as Christ accepted
you, in order to bring praise to God.

DO YOU DISCRIMINATE?

Although discrimination takes place in other settings, employment-related discrimination is by far the most reported act of unfairness. This is the case primarily for two reasons: one, the result is usually a financial disparity, and two, it is one that can be tracked or proven by a paper trail (for example, resumes, employment applications, performance reviews, interoffice memos, etc.).

We should be aware of these acts because they may happen to us—or we may be directed by a company policy or boss to commit one of these discriminatory actions. Or we may inadvertently commit discrimination ourselves—it can happen easily if we aren't aware of what is considered discriminatory.

So what would be considered discriminatory? The list includes: 1. Not advertising job openings in newspapers that reach a particular demographic group. 2. Looking at the address of an applicant and making assumptions about the person. 3. Attempting to determine race based upon the college listed on the resume. 4. Making hiring decisions based upon how a qualified person would fit in with other employees who are different. 5. Thinking that there are too many men or women and that the company needs some balance. 6. Assuming that a person's previous illness or handicap will keep him from performing the job. 7. Thinking that a woman with several children will lose too much time from the office because of family issues. 8. Requiring a photograph to be submitted with an application so everyone will know what the person looks like even before reviewing qualifications. 9. Conducting an unauthorized credit check on the applicant to obtain information that is not normally contained on an application and not pertinent to the job. 10. Advertising executive or "white collar" positions in select newspapers or making them available only through headhunters. 11. Delegating gender-based tasks. 12. Wanting the applicant to have a particular "company look." 13. Noting weight, hairstyles, and other personal or physical characteristics.

Some of these practices have become so common that we may not even realize that they are discriminatory. Anything that is used to disqualify a person for a job, raise, or promotion is discriminatory. Even carrying on a conversation, whether or not we initiated it, with a superior about a coworker can result in an unfair practice against that person.

We need to keep in mind that the next people talked about could be us and the topic could be our Christian beliefs. We must guard ourselves from the trickery and deceptive practices that surround us in the world of work and pray that our employers will be fair with everyone.

_____

Respecting Diversity: From the beginning God did not plan for us to all be the same. After all, He created man and then woman. The Old Testament even identifies Israelites and Gentile people as different, but He loved them the same. Diversity was part of God's plans from the beginning. So, as a Christian, you must recognize and accept that diversity is God's desire—one that you should not disrespect. God has given us all a fair and equal chance and He expects us to do the same for each other.

Morning Prayer

Almighty God, help me to accept and embrace with a spirit of love all those whom you have created to carry out Your divine plans on earth. Lord, I ask that I look at everyone as a child of Yours and as my brother and sister. If I should stray today in my respect and love for everyone, I pray that the Holy Spirit will prick my heart to bring about love, repentance, and forgiveness. Amen.

OPENING THE SHADES AND REMOVING THE BLINDERS

- If you see an injustice, don't remain silent; speak up for what is right. Ask God to give you strength, courage, and wisdom. You are morally accountable for every wrong which you could have prevented.

- Think about how you felt when as a child no one wanted to play with you.

- Those who discriminate show how far they are from God. Many people who discriminate are simply showing their own lack of security and how little peace they have with themselves.

- Discrimination is one way the devil divides. Remember the phrase "divide and conquer." If we are not together, we can never conquer the world and workplace for Christ.

- We are made in God's likeness, so when you discriminate against someone, you are mistreating God.

- Let your lifestyle and actions promote universal love, acceptance, and concern. God calls you to stand for righteousness even when you are in the minority. Stand up for His Word, knowing that He will see you through.

- God unites you with brothers and sisters with different backgrounds, interests, challenges, and destinies. We are all one in Christ.

- As a Christian, you are probably a minority at your job. Should you be discriminated against because you are different than most of the others?

- As God's children, we are all pleasing to His eyes.God sees no difference between those of different skin colors, those with or without college degrees, or those who live in a particular part of town—so why should you? Move past what is on the surface and embrace what God sees— magnificent creations each with a specific purpose. God looks at the heart—including yours.

Evening Prayer

Father God, I pray that You will help me fight discrimination—both in myself and in others. Make my own life an example of how You want Your children to treat each other. If it is Your will, please use me in this way. Amen.

SCRIPTURE REFERENCES

John 13:34-35

A new command I give you: Love one another. As I have loved you, so you must love one another. By this all men will know that you are my disciples, if you love one another.

1 Samuel 16:7

But the Lord said to Samuel, "Do not consider his appearance or his height. . . .The Lord does not look at the things man looks at. . . .the Lord looks at the heart."

1 John 3:11

This is the message you heard from the beginning: We should love one another.

James 2:1-4

My brothers, as believers in our glorious Lord Jesus Christ, don't show favoritism. Suppose a man comes into your meeting wearing a gold ring and fine clothes, and a poor man in shabby clothes also comes in. If you show special attention to the man wearing fine clothes and say, "Here's a good seat for you," but say to the poor man, "You stand there" or "Sit on the floor by my feet," have you not discriminated among yourselves and become judges with evil thoughts?

Romans 12:3-5

For by the grace given me I say to every one of you: Do not think of yourself more highly than you ought, but rather think of yourself with sober judgment, in accordance with the measure of faith God has given you. Just as each of us has one body with many members, and these members do not all have the same function, so in Christ we who are many form one body, and each member belongs to all the others.

1 Peter 1:22

Now that you have purified yourselves by obeying the truth so that you have sincere love for your brothers, love one another deeply, from the heart.

1 Peter 3:8

Finally, all of you, live in harmony with one another; be sympathetic, love as brothers, be compassionate and humble.

1 John 2:9-11

Anyone who claims to be in the light but hates his brother is still in the darkness. Whoever loves his brother lives in the light, and there is nothing in him to make him stumble. But whoever hates his brother is in the darkness and walks around in the darkness; he does not know where he is going, because the darkness has blinded him.

DISMISSAL

Fired, furloughed, downsized, laid off,
    whatever it's called,
        you lost your job this week.
Your human side starts to make you worry
    about the next job you will seek.
Cast those concerns aside,
God promises to provide!
It is not over, it may be a new beginning
    because you never know what God is sending.
Don't look just for a job.
Look for the opportunity to serve God!

Quick Script: Matthew 6:33-34

But seek first his kingdom and his righteousness, and all these things will be given to you
as well. Therefore do not worry about tomorrow, for tomorrow will worry about itself. Each
day has enough trouble of its own.

Lose a Job, Not Your Spirit!

Some of us lose a job and act as if we have lost our best friend—Jesus. We seem to think that He has abandoned us by allowing something this unpleasant into our lives.

We've forgotten, though, that it was the Holy Spirit who directed us to our job in the first place, and He had a specific purpose for us there. Besides, it was never "our" job; we don't have ownership over anything.

Instead, we have much more! We have the plan that God has for our life and we have the Holy Spirit to guide us along that path toward eternity. Along the way, there will be stops, twists, and turns—and every one of them already planned, each with something for us to do and learn.

When God decides that it is time to take the next step, then He pushes us along by closing some doors and opening others. We don't like it when a door slams shut in our face; not many people start singing and praising God when they lose a job. But we have to keep things in perspective—God's perspective. If our focus is on being available to take another step along the path toward eternity, we will find comfort in knowing that God is in charge, and He will never abandon us.

If we are patient, He will open another door, directing us on to where He wants us next.

God Always Has a Job for You: As a child of Christ, you have the important job of spreading the gospel, setting an example for others, helping others in need, loving everyone, and following Jesus' example. The importance of this job far outweighs any man-created job. We work for God, first and foremost!

Morning Prayer

Heavenly Father, as I prepare for my day this morning help me to focus first on what You have asked me to do. Let me not place any other tasks in front of Your requests. And if I experience any change in my employment or surroundings, I ask for an unclouded vision to bring my thoughts back to the Bible and Your promises. In faith, I know everything will be all right. In Jesus' name, I pray. Amen.

WORKING FOR GOD

- Even when losing what seems like everything, remember you have the riches of faith, love, and salvation.

- Although things may seem unfair, realize that God has a reason for what happened. If you believe and trust, you will await the next opportunity. When changes occur, God has a better plan.

- When looking back, you may see that all along you were where you should not have been and that this was the only way to change your course.

- If your actions merited your dismissal, you have to admit and accept the consequences of your actions. Look at the total situation and see where you may have gone wrong. It can't always be someone else's fault. Take this opportunity to learn from your mistakes and to make the best of what you experienced as you move on.

- This, too, like everything else, will pass. Eventually, it will be history, becoming a distant memory.

- Rid yourself of the false measure of job success; only God can measure your success.

- Remember, God gives us trials in our lives to build

us up, not tear us down. Sometimes God breaks us so He can remake us.

- Don't waste time wondering Why me? or How could you? Instead, ask What's next? and make yourself available. Thank God for what He has in store next, and wait on Him to bring it about.

- Many life-changing events in the Bible occurred when someone was on the way to another place.

- God's work—and your life—are not over just because your job has ended.

- Leave tomorrow prayerfully and faithfully in God's hands. He will supply.

Evening Prayer

Father God, I ask for Your direction so that I may clearly see that I am doing Your work. I release myself to You for Your use, regardless of where You put me. I open my arms to embrace the opportunities available to me now through the changes I have experienced. Father, please be with me. Amen.

Scripture References

Psalm 140: 1-5

Rescue me, O Lord, from evil men; protect me from men of violence, who devise evil plans in their hearts and stir up war every day. They make their tongues as sharp as a serpent's; the poison of vipers is on their lips. Keep me, O Lord, from the hands of the wicked; protect me from men of violence who plan to trip my feet. Proud men have hidden a snare for me; they have spread out the cords of their net and have set traps for me along my path.

Psalm 107:1

Give thanks to the Lord, for he is good; his love endures forever.

Jeremiah 29:11

"For I know the plans I have for you," declares the Lord, "plans to prosper you and not to harm you, plans to give you hope and a future."

Ephesians 6:10-12

Finally, be strong in the Lord and in his mighty power. Put on the full armor of God so that you can take your stand against the devil's schemes. For our struggle is not against flesh and blood, but against the rulers, against the authorities, against the powers of this dark world and against the spiritual forces of evil in the heavenly realms.

Habakkuk 3:17-18

Though the fig tree does not bud and there are no grapes on the vines, though the olive crop fails and the fields produce no food, though there are no sheep in the pen and no cattle in the stalls, yet I will rejoice in the Lord, I will be joyful in God my Savior.

Romans 8:35-39

Who shall separate us from the love of Christ? Shall trouble or hardship or persecution or famine or nakedness or danger or sword? As it is written: "For your sake we face death all day long; we are considered as sheep to be slaughtered." No, in all these things we are more than conquerors through him who loved us. For I am convinced that neither death nor life, neither angels nor demons, neither the present nor the future, nor any powers, neither height nor depth, nor anything else in all creation, will be able to separate us from the love of God that is in Christ Jesus our Lord.

Jeremiah 18:5-6

Then the word of the Lord came to me: "O house of Israel, can I not do with you as this potter does?" declares the Lord. "Like the clay in the hand of the potter, so are you in my hand. . . ."

2 Corinthians 5:7

We live by faith, not by sight.

EDUCATION

Some have read hundreds of books,
   while others hang certificates on hooks.
Some insist on being called professor,
   then look down on others as "lesser."
They may have gone to college,
   but have they read the Book of Knowledge?
Then there are those with advanced degrees,
   obsessed with catching misplaced "I's" or
      uncrossed "t's."
Some may think to have status you must have
      higher education,
   but they really are full of a bunch of
      misinformation.
God created us all equal and that is what applies,
   because we are all the same in God's eyes.

Quick Script: Romans 1:22

Although they claimed to be wise, they became
fools.

The Miseducation of the Masses

Were you told that you would not "amount" to anything unless you went to college? If you stepped out of line in school, were you told you would end up like the "lazy, no-account" drunkard on the street? If you chose to pursue a trade instead of college, did people say you just weren't college material—whatever that means? If you decided to attend community college, was it assumed that you were not accepted at a four-year college? Then, when you went to college, if it was not one of the big-name schools, they thought you just couldn't get in one of the ones deemed prestigious. After undergraduate school you de-cided to go to work right away, finding out a couple of years later that the company preferred employees with advanced degrees. So you decided to attend school at night. You lost time with your family and friends, along with a lot of sleep. Finally you got your advanced degree and expected something to happen. Nothing changed and you realized it really didn't matter. Now the company was hiring kids right out of school, because they would work for less money. Then, you heard about potential reductions in the workforce and that they were going to get rid of the people who had been there the longest and made the most money. You now fell into both of those categories. Then you wondered how you got caught up in this maze.

Hopefully, your thoughts will turn both to the Bible and to history. Many of our great historical and biblical leaders were common people without formal educations.

God gives everyone abilities, talents, and gifts. When you use those, nothing around you can make you feel inferior, regardless of what level of education or job you have. Keep your head up and remain strong. Feel secure in doing what God wants you to do, not what others are doing.

Education for Life: The best source of learning is the Bible. In it you will find all you need to know to live, work, and thrive. Of course you have to receive some formal education. But the key to living fully and happily, regardless of your education level, is found in the pages of your Bible. When you get a twinge of "I should have" or "I wish I had," pick up your Bible and read that God is the One who directs your path.

Father God, I pray for Your guidance in helping me to focus on Your work today, doing it to the best of my ability. Help me never forget that I am precious in Your sight and You accept me as I am. I am not less than anyone else, nor am I better— we all are the same in Your eyes. Help me to use the gifts You have given me to Your glory. Lord, I pray that I will neither try to compete with others nor look down on others. Amen.

ACKNOWLEDGE THE KNOWLEDGE FROM ABOVE

- God can hear your prayers even if you don't pronounce every word correctly or use perfect grammar.

- God's message is for people of all educational levels.

- Pursuing education is often a good idea, but don't let it give you a false sense of security or an unrealistic self-reliance on your own abilities. If you lean on your degree, you may fall on your lack of faith.

- To know our life's plan, we must know the Lord. Life's primary purpose is to know and serve God.

Learning about Him is the education we most need as Christians.

- •There's no knowledge greater than that found in the Bible. Biblical education is the only way to be set free from error, worry, and other worldly concerns.

- •You get a failing grade if you judge someone based upon their education.

- •The only "Master" of anything is God.

- •God has and will continue to equip you to accomplish His will. Rely upon Him.

———————

Evening Prayer

Dear Heavenly Father, I give thanks to You for providing me with everything I needed today to make it through another workday. When I thought I couldn't handle the task, You stepped in and gave the resources I needed. I know that I need Your presence in my life more than I need any degree or status that worldly education could give me. Lord, I submit myself to You. I know You will see me through. Amen.

SCRIPTURE REFERENCES

Psalm 119:137-144

Righteous are you, O Lord, and your laws are right. The statutes you have laid down are righteous; they are fully trustworthy. My zeal wears me out, for my enemies ignore your words. Your promises have been thoroughly tested, and your servant loves them. Though I am lowly and despised, I do not forget your precepts. Your righteousness is everlasting and your law is true. Trouble and distress have come upon me, but your commands are my delight. Your statutes are forever right; give me understanding that I may live.

Proverbs 24:5

A wise man has great power, and a man of knowledge increases strength.

Proverbs 12:9

Better to be a nobody and yet have a servant than pretend to be somebody and have no food.

Proverbs 11:28

Whoever trusts in his riches will fall, but the righteous will thrive like a green leaf.

1 Corinthians 3:7-9

So neither he who plants nor he who waters is anything, but only God, who makes things grow. The man who plants and the man who waters have one purpose, and each will be rewarded according to his own labor. For we are God's fellow workers; you are God's field, God's building.

Philippians 4:12-13

I know what it is to be in need, and I know what it is to have plenty. I have learned the secret of being content in any and every situation, whether well fed or hungry, whether living in plenty or in want. I can do everything through him who gives me strength.

2 Peter 3:18

But grow in the grace and knowledge of our Lord and Savior Jesus Christ. To him be glory both now and forever! Amen.

ENVY

Are you happy when others get promotions,
or does the devil bring out jealous emotions?
Do you congratulate sincerely
or think that you deserved it really?
Do you compare what they have gained
to what you have or haven't obtained?
Have you forgotten all God has done for you,
forgetting how prayer made your dreams
come true?
Do you remember that God has a plan
for what He wants for every woman and man?
Do not get distracted by earthly reward,
because heaven awaits as your award.

Quick Script: 1 Corinthians 13:4

Love is patient, love is kind. It does not envy, it
does not boast, it is not proud.

. . . is obviously not what God intends for us; otherwise we would have the same things. We may realize this reality; but we are pressured by children, spouses, parents, and coworkers to have and to give "things" that mean absolutely nothing to the Kingdom of God.

Although we try to protect our children and raise them the right way, they still will ask for the latest toy or the new trend in clothes. When we ask them why they want these things, we usually get the same response—because someone else has them. Envy begins early, even as toddlers, when one child wants what another child is holding. This is when we need to begin to teach our children about sharing and about being happy with what we have in our own hands.

Our spouses, although they usually know better, aren't immune to an occasional twinge of envy either. Perhaps we have not gone out to dinner lately, haven't had a vacation in a couple of years, still have furniture from when we were first married—all the things that we have been brainwashed into thinking make a marriage successful. Then our neighbors gladly keep us up-to-date on their trips, new cars, and gadgets. We should be happy for them, remembering to be thankful for what God has provided our household.

Our parents, with good intentions, want the best for us. Through some measuring stick that only they know, they assess our lives, wanting us to do better than they did with their careers. So they ask about our job status, chance for promotion, and interest in changing professions, all along thinking about what their friends' children are doing with their professional lives. If we don't measure up on that measuring stick of theirs, our parents wish for better "things" for us. We should gently let them know that we are content with our life because we have the Holy Spirit with us each day, guiding us according to God's plan.

Coworkers don't understand why we don't go after someone's job because we would be better off, why we befriend the new boss, and how we can be happy when others have been promoted. What they don't realize is that we are where God wants us until He is ready to move us.

Envious attitudes are contagious. All too easily we absorb these feelings from those around us, and all too easily we pass them along to others. To deal with envy, we have to always remember that we have the greatest possessions of all: salvation, God, and eternal life. Nothing else is necessary, and nothing else can compare.

———————

Envy Invites Unrest: There's no way for you to have any peace and rest if you are concerned about the worldly goods of someone else. Be at peace with what you have, knowing God will always provide for your needs—even if He doesn't always give you your "wants."

Most honorable Father God, I pray today that You'll remind me to be thankful for all that You have provided for me. I know that You have a plan for me unlike any others. I pray for Your help in keeping me focused on our relationship and not on things that have no place in Your Kingdom. Amen.

KEEPING EVERYTHING IN FOCUS

- God did not create each of us to have the same life or the same things. You will never be happy if you think you should have the same things as someone else.

- We must honor God's plans and not be resentful or envious of His plans for others.

- Wanting what someone else has is dangerous! You may get it and fall out of God's will and into the hands of the devil.

- Can you manage everything you have already?

- How many "things" have you accumulated that have been tossed out, never used, or are simply dust collectors?

- Envy clouds your eyes to what you need versus what you want, and most important, what God wants you to have at this time.

- Learn to be satisfied with all that you have been given. Have you taken an inventory of what you do have before counting what you think you should have now?

- Sometimes if you have a little patience, you may be blessed with what you want. The important thing is to wait on God. But if you want things for the wrong reasons, you may never get them—and if you get things for the wrong reasons, those things may be the source of an ongoing desire for more that could grow out of control.

- The deceitfulness of riches and the desire for things bring destruction to your faithfulness.

- You can always lose your possessions, but not your God-given qualities and salvation. Focus on enriching your life spiritually rather than with material things and man-made titles.

• Look to people who have peace, love, and a giving nature. These are the things you should strive to obtain, and these are the people you should long to be like.

———

Evening Prayer

Heavenly Father, I praise Your name tonight as I thank You for giving me the security of being who I am, with what I have, and doing what I do. I thank You because I know that all things come from You and without You I would be lost, aimlessly wandering, trying to be different, better, bigger, or higher. I am different because I have You in my heart. Amen.

———

SCRIPTURE REFERENCES

Hebrews 13:5
Keep your lives free from the love of money and be content with what you have, because God has said, "Never will I leave you; never will I forsake you."

Exodus 20:17

You shall not covet your neighbor's house. You shall not covet your neighbor's wife, or his manservant or maidservant, his ox or donkey, or anything that belongs to your neighbor.

Romans 13:12-14

The night is nearly over; the day is almost here. So let us put aside the deeds of darkness and put on the armor of light. Let us behave decently, as in the daytime, not in orgies and drunkenness, not in sexual immorality and debauchery, not in dissension and jealousy. Rather, clothe yourselves with the Lord Jesus Christ, and do not think about how to gratify the desires of the sinful nature.

Matthew 20:12-16

"These men who were hired last worked only one hour," they said, "and you have made them equal to us who have borne the burden of the work and the heat of the day." But he answered one of them, "Friend, I am not being unfair to you. Didn't you agree to work for a denarius? Take your pay and go. I want to give the man who was hired last the same as I gave you. Don't I have the right to do what I want with my own money? Or, are you envious because I am generous? So the last will be first, and the first will be last."

Matthew 6:22-23

The eye is the lamp of the body. If your eyes are good, your whole body will be full of light. But if your eyes are bad, your whole body will be full of darkness. If then the light within you is darkness, how great is that darkness!

Psalm 49:16-20

Do not be overawed when a man grows rich, when the splendor of his house increases; for he will take nothing with him when he dies, his splendor will not descend with him. Though while he lived he counted himself blessed—and men praise you when you prosper—he will join the generation of his fathers, who will never see the light of life. A man who has riches without understanding is like the beasts that perish.

Philippians 4:12-13

I know what it is to be in need, and I know what it is to have plenty. I have learned the secret of being content in any and every situation, whether well fed or hungry, whether living in plenty or in want. I can do everything through him who gives me strength.

FEAR

It started with layoffs and rumors of shutdown.
If I lose my job, what will I do in this town?
Then they said our benefits would be cut.
I'll be the first one to get sick, with my luck.
If my wife or child are ill,
   how will I pay the bill?
Now I'm getting a new boss,
I'm not sure if this is a gain or a loss.
I've heard stories about his loud commands
   and his unreasonable demands.
I really don't know what to expect,
   except I better show the utmost respect.
I was tossing and turning all night,
   restless, wide awake, and full of fright.
Then I kneeled down to pray with all my might,
   and God let me know everything was all right.

Quick Script: Psalm 56:3-4

When I am afraid, I will trust in you. In God,
whose word I praise, in God I trust; I will not
be afraid. What can mortal man do to me?

Faith Conquers Fear

When we allow fear to enter our lives, we kick faith right outside our mind's door. In fact, we almost *lose* our minds with all of the "what-ifs" and "buts." Fear is the devil's weapon against Christ's peace.

We need to kick fear out and let faith back in. We don't know what God has planned for us—but He will reveal it according to His schedule. Meanwhile, we have the assurance of something far more important than a job: our salvation.

So why do we let little things like a new boss, a re-structuring, different policies, or a job change consume our thoughts? We should stop and think, and then look to see what God is doing for us and what He wants us to do. Maybe we have been resisting His command and He had to take some action to get us moving. Pos-sibly some-one needs our help and God needs to bring us in contact with that person. Or He may be bringing someone into our lives to further our own spiritual growth. We must look at the situation and ask ourselves, "What does God want me to do?" If it is not apparent to us, then we need to ask God for guidance. Otherwise, we may make a bad decision that will lead us away from our purpose on earth.

Have we accepted and quit jobs without praying first? Have we moved from city to city, job to job, and still remained unhappy? Actions taken or not taken because of fear may be keeping us from a blessing. Sometimes we have to remain still, let things happen around us, and then let God take the lead.

When He leads, then we must follow. He'll show us the right path to take in our career. He certainly will not leave us now, when He's been with us all along. We must simply remember to put our faith and patience in action—instead of reacting out of fear.

———————

Good Fear and Bad Fear: Fear can be healthy; it can keep you away from dangers and steer you toward the right path. But fear can also paralyze. Don't remain confused by bad fear; you can't do anything if you are so afraid that you question the outcome of any action you want to take. Keep your faith and get rid of the fear that paralyzes; turn to God and He'll show you how to go. The best fear is the fear of God.

———————

Most gracious and honorable Father, I ask You to help me stay focused on the Holy Spirit as my guide, facing any situation at work with confidence, security, and peace, while knowing that with You I have nothing to fear. You are the greatest conqueror. Amen.

FREEDOM FROM FEAR

•Fear fades when you trust your Father. God provides peace in the midst of turmoil, and He protects His children.

•God knows your concerns; you are not alone.

•If you have to fear something, be afraid of not following God's will.

•Fear can paralyze your feet and keep you from walking on the path God plans.

•We experience true peace and freedom when we refuse to listen to fear's lies.

- Why be afraid of what may never happen? Only one Person knows the future and you can trust Him! Do you find you often spend time being afraid of things over which we have absolutely no control? God is going to work it all out anyway, so you might as well relax.

- When you completely surrender to God, when you let go and let God take total control—then you will have no more fear.

- You can face any difficult situation with confidence if you are a faithful child of God.

Evening Prayer

Dear Lord in heaven, I thank You for being my savior and protector at all times, whether I'm awake or asleep. When I feel fear, it is comforting to know You are always near. Help me, Father, to remove the emotion of fear through total devotion to You in everything that I do. Amen.

SCRIPTURE REFERENCES

Psalm 31:14-15

But I trust in you, O Lord; I say, "You are my God." My times are in your hands; deliver me from my enemies and from those who pursue me.

Psalm 34:9

Fear the Lord, you his saints, for those who fear him lack nothing.

Psalm 34:19-20

A righteous man may have many troubles, but the Lord delivers him from them all; he protects all his bones, not one of them will be broken.

Psalm 57:2-3

I cry out to God Most High, to God, who fulfills his purpose for me. He sends from heaven and saves me, rebuking those who hotly pursue me; God sends his love and his faithfulness.

Luke 6:27-31

"But I tell you who hear me: Love your enemies, do good to those who hate you, bless those who curse you, pray for those who mistreat you. If someone strikes you on one cheek, turn to him the other also. If someone takes your cloak, do not stop him from taking your tunic. Give to everyone who asks you, and if anyone takes what belongs to you, do not demand it back. Do to others as you would have them do to you.

Psalm 46:1-3

God is our refuge and strength, an ever-present help in trouble. Therefore we will not fear, though the earth give way and the mountains fall into the heart of the sea, though its waters roar and foam and the mountains quake with their surging.

2 Timothy 1:7

For God did not give us a spirit of timidity, but a spirit of power, of love and of self-discipline.

Hebrews 12:1-3

Therefore, since we are surrounded by such a great cloud of witnesses, let us throw off everything that hinders and the sin that so easily entangles, and let us run with perseverance the race marked out for us. Let us fix our eyes on Jesus, the author and perfecter of our faith, who for the joy set before him endured the cross, scorning its shame, and sat down at the right hand of the throne of God. Consider him who endured such opposition from sinful men, so that you will not grow weary and lose heart.

Psalm 112:1

Praise the Lord. Blessed is the man who fears the Lord, who finds great delight in his commands.

Psalm 50:15

And call upon me in the day of trouble; I will deliver you, and you will honor me.

FRIENDSHIPS

Maybe you've had one
   since you were small.
That special friend
   with whom you share all.
Or now that you're grown,
   maybe you have even more to share.
Work is complicated and you need to talk
   to someone who will understand and care.
Your coworker has a confidential, listening ear,
   she knows what you are going through
   as you reveal your thoughts and fear.
Other colleagues say things and stare,
   wondering and assuming what might be said.
Don't let them keep you from your friend,
   usually they are just afraid you may get ahead.
Through the petty jealousy and suspicion,
   keep your friendship true and strong.
Remember, that special friend, whether old or new,
   was intended by God for you all along.

———————

Quick Script: Proverbs 18:24

A man of many companions may come to ruin,
but there is a friend who sticks closer than a
brother.

CAN FRIENDS WORK TOGETHER?

Yes, we can be friends and work together also! But separating the friendship from the work takes a little discipline, especially if we work in the same department, have the same job, report to the same person, or one reports to the other.

Often people will say the worst people to work with are family and friends. That's a little ironic since these are the people we usually trust the most. We trust them with taking care of our children, staying in our home when we go out of town, and borrowing our car.

However, working together can destroy a relationship if we are not careful. We may think, "We've been friends for years, our friendship can withstand anything" —but when our boss tells us something in confidence and our friend wants to know what was said, should we tell or keep it to ourselves? When we know someone is about to be fired, do we reveal it to our friend? If our friend suspects that we know something, does she try to get us to reveal what we've been told? What happens if we don't? What if our friend applies for the same newly created position that we do? How will we respond if she gets the position? These are just some of the strains that working together puts on a friendship.

These are pretty touchy issues, ones that could jeopardize our friendships. But in the midst of these types of circumstances we have to put God first and not act out of emotion. Emotional acts can cause us to do things to fall out of God's favor—and we may jeopardize our friendship. In every case, apply biblical principles and make sure you do what God wants. Whether your friend is a Christian or not, she will respect your obedience and standards.

—————

Features of a Friend: A true friend should treat you as God treats us. A true friend is: forgiving, accepting, caring, inspiring, teaching, correcting, comforting, and loving. A true friend is always there for you with a listening ear, a soft heart, and words of wisdom. A true friend lets you know if you've done something wrong. A true friend is someone in whom you can place all of your trust. God is your first true Friend—do you have another?

—————

Morning Prayer

Dear Father, I pray for my friends today, for You to comfort them in their concerns, uncertainties, and whatever they may face today. I ask You, Lord, for wisdom for the proper words and actions to be a good friend. I pray, too, that I will act without hesitation to respond to my friend's needs. Amen.

The Friendship Formula

- Friends love one another at all times.

- Friendship is not contingent upon if the relationship is profitable in some way.

- Being a true friend requires you to tell the truth even when it hurts.

- Your friendship with others must be an enduring one, especially in times of adversity. Constancy and consistency are essential elements in genuine friendships. Use your friendship with God as an example. He is loyal, always there, and a confidant.

- Close friends can increase the joy of your life, even in the workplace.

- In friendship you have support—independence and self-reliance is not God's plan for you.

- God wants you to be genuinely interested in the problems of others and to have a willing ear for troubled souls. You should respond to people and treat them as Jesus did.

- Ask God to show you the person He wants you to serve, and do it graciously in love.

- In a world of people who could care less, you should care more.

- Don't put pressure on your friends to be the same type of friend that you are to them.

- All friendships are not designed to last forever. When one ends or changes, realize that God is making room for another person to enter your life or for you to reach another.

- Don't take your friendship lightly; it may be all that the other person has right now.

- Friends hurt each other's feelings, but your Friend in heaven will never hurt you if you turn to Him in your times of need.

- Don't place earthly friendships higher than God. Above all, He is your ultimate Friend and Companion. People cannot help but fail each other sometimes, but He will always be there.

———————

Heavenly Father, I thank You for the friends You have placed in my life to help me with my challenges and to share in my joy. I pray, Lord, that I will be as good a friend to them as they have been to me and that together we can grow in our relationship with You, our Father. Amen.

SCRIPTURE REFERENCES

Genesis 2:18
The Lord God said, "It is not good for the man to be alone. I will make a helper suitable for him."

Proverbs 17:17
A friend loves at all times, and a brother is born for adversity.

Proverbs 13:20
He who walks with the wise grows wise, but a companion of fools suffers harm.

Galatians 6:1-2

Brothers, if someone is caught in a sin, you who are spiritual should restore him gently. But, watch yourself, or you also may be tempted. Carry each other's burdens, and in this way you will fulfill the law of Christ.

Gossip

It doesn't need to be passed on, even if it's true.
Remember, the next rumor could be about you.
If you listen to ridicule and scoop,
    you'll become part of the vicious loop.
Keep confidential the things you were told,
    those things you've promised to withhold.
Move away from those who point fingers and talk.
Don't jeopardize your Christian walk.
If you slip up along the way,
    pray to God for control in what you say.

———

Quick Script: Proverbs 11:9

With his mouth the godless destroys his neighbor, but through knowledge the righteous escape.

———

Bringing the Rumor Mill
to a Grinding Halt

Sometimes we encounter someone who always has some "news" to share. This sort of person seems to thrive on knowing it all. They may simply be misguided, thinking that they are doing a favor by sharing confidential information. Or they may have malice in their heart.

As a Christian, how should we respond? First, we should be honest and say we are uncomfortable with this sort of conversation. If the person is a Christian, remind him gently of God's dislike of gossiping. He may not even realize that what he is doing is gossiping.

Nobody is perfect, but if the person refuses to change his conversations with us, we may need to evaluate if this is a person with whom we should associate. If we feel God does want us in this person's life, then we can help him control his tongue instead of letting it flap like a thirsty dog's. We can challenge him by saying, "Let's talk to our coworker about this together," or "If I can't tell our manager what you said, then it's something I really don't want to know." Let him know when he has used harsh and condemning words. Ask him how he would feel if someone was sharing *his* personal information. When talking with him, point out the positive in situations and in people. Don't be shy; tell him that you think he was wrong to say what he said.

The goal is to get him to realize how gossip affects his relationship with others. In the long run, though, we can't change others—only Christ can do that. We are each responsible before God for our own behavior, and we must be careful to keep ourselves free from gossip's chains.

Power to Destroy: We should use the great power of our minds and mouths to build others up instead of cutting them down. Think about what you are about to say before you speak. Does it help or hurt? Is it necessary? How will others be affected? Use the blessing of speech that God gave to give blessings to others.

Morning Prayer:

Heavenly Father, I thank You for giving me the ability to speak and I pray that You will help me to use my gift for You. Be with me, Lord, as I try to use my words to comfort and encourage. Help me to make a difference in someone's life. Amen.

Hear No Evil, Speak No Evil

- Let the words from your mouth be acceptable to God. Is what you said pleasing to God's ears?

- Guard your words and actions so you will not offend or hurt anyone.

- God gave us the ability to talk to spread His gospel and good will—not to gossip.

- If you cannot speak kindly, remain silent.

- Be sympathetic and prayerful, not judgmental. Look for the good in everyone, instead of criticizing one of God's children.

- Pass on your joy and love to those with whom you work, instead of passing along someone's misfortune. Counter destructive news with good.

- Turn away when others start to gossip and pray for the determination not to repeat what you hear.

- Criticize less and praise more. Use the power of your tongue to build others up, instead of tearing them down.

Lord, I give all honor and glory to You as You brought me through another workday. Guard me always against the temptation to hurt anyone with my words; may I instead be filled with the desire to show Your love and joy. I pray that my words today made someone's day a little brighter and a step closer to knowing You as their Father. Amen.

SCRIPTURE REFERENCES

Proverbs 25:18
Like a club or a sword or a sharp arrow is the man who gives false testimony against his neighbor.

Psalm 57:4
I am in the midst of lions; I lie among ravenous beasts—men whose teeth are spears and arrows, whose tongues are sharp swords.

Exodus 23:1
Do not spread false reports. Do not help a wicked man by being a malicious witness.

Psalm 39:1

I said, "I will watch my ways and keep my tongue from sin; I will put a muzzle on my mouth as long as the wicked are in my presence."

Proverbs 10:19

When words are many, sin is not absent, but he who holds his tongue is wise.

2 Thessalonians 3:11-12

We hear that some among you are idle. They are not busy; they are busybodies. Such people we command and urge in the Lord Jesus Christ to settle down and earn the bread they eat.

Proverbs 21:23

He who guards his mouth and his tongue keeps himself from calamity.

James 3:5-6

Likewise the tongue is a small part of the body, but it makes great boasts. Consider what a great forest is set on fire by a small spark. The tongue also is a fire, a world of evil among the parts of the body. It corrupts the whole person, sets the whole course of his life on fire, and is itself set on fire by hell.

Ephesians 4:29

Do not let any unwholesome talk come out of

your mouths, but only what is helpful for building others up according to their needs, that it may benefit those who listen.

Psalm 35:28
My tongue will speak of your righteousness and of your praises all day long.

Isaiah 58:9-10
If you do away with the yoke of oppression, with the pointing finger and malicious talk, and if you spend yourselves in behalf of the hungry and satisfy the needs of the oppressed, then your light will rise in the darkness, and your night will become like the noonday.

JOBS

You may not like the days or hours
   or what you have to do,
      but you are where God placed you.
You want to do more
      because you have the skill,
         yet you have to follow God's will.
You have grown impatient
      waiting on a new position,
         but maybe you haven't yet completed your
         mission.
You don't feel appreciated
      for all that you have done,
         but what's most important is pleasing the
         Holy One.

Quick Script: Colossians 3:17

And whatever you do, whether in word or deed,
do it all in the name of the Lord Jesus, giving
thanks to God the Father through him.

WORKING IT OUT

There's so much in life that we think we have to work out ourselves. We have to find a job, make sure it's the right job, make enough money to provide for our families, fit in with the corporate environment, try to move up in the company, deal with a coworker who is not friendly, handle the demands of an unreasonable boss, do the job of two or three people, and perform tasks that go against our ethical and moral beliefs. In the process of all of these things, we simply forget to take God to work with us.

We leave God at home after we finish our morning devotionals, keeping Him from helping us deal with the tests and trials of the day. Then we go home and pray about something that perhaps would not have happened, a situation that we could have handled differently if we had been relying on God all through the day. What we don't do is to call upon God while we are at work, when we have decisions to make, when we are uncomfortable, when we are dealing with people, and when we are facing challenges.

Let God work things out. He is available to help if you only call upon Him.

The Real Corporate Giant: God is the real "corporate giant." He is also the perfect boss because He is always available, He listens, He gives direction, and He supplies all of our needs. So, before we try to take on the corporation all by ourselves, consult with the Boss on high.

Morning Prayer

In the name of Jesus, I come to You this morning, Father, to thank You first for the job that You have provided. I pray that I will do my work diligently because that is what gives You joy. I anxiously await the tasks before me today with a desire to perform them well. Amen.

WORK WITH WISDOM

• Do not conform to the world's ways, but instead seek the approval of God through your thoughts and actions.

- When we perform the work God has given us, it is rewarding to us and others in ways we don't often see.

- There is no need to feel inadequate for the work God has given you because He has given you the strength and power you need to complete the task.

- Look at every task as a blessed experience from God, no matter what it may appear to be on the surface. Every experience is part of your spiritual growth.

- Approach every task as if God Himself asked you personally to do the job.

- Your attitude toward work will dictate your productivity and feelings. Have the attitude of a fruitful servant ready to produce good work.

- No matter how small or large the project, approach it with the same level of importance. Everything we do is seen by God. Don't let Him see laziness, half-hearted efforts, and sloppiness.

- When you feel that there is just not enough time to do what you have to do, let God's love and power move through you to renew and strengthen you.

- It is so easy for you to say "I can't," but God blesses you when you give your best effort.

- Remember, He sent that task for you to handle.

- For every task, someone has to do it—what makes you above doing any task? Even when the work appears unappealing, know that God is with you and do it to please Him.

———————

Evening Prayer

Heavenly Father, You brought me through another day and I thank You for all that You did for me today. Lord, I know that none of what I did was done alone. I give You all the glory, praise, and honor for working through me and equipping me for the work done today. Amen.

———————

SCRIPTURE REFERENCES

Ephesians 4:28
He who has been stealing must steal no longer, but must work, doing something useful with his own hands, that he may have something to share with those in need.

2 Thessalonians 3:10
For even when we were with you, we gave you this rule: "If a man will not work, he shall not eat."

1 Thessalonians 4:11-12
Make it your ambition to lead a quiet life, to mind your own business and to work with your hands, just as we told you, so that your daily life may win the respect of outsiders and so that you will not be dependent on anybody.

Ecclesiastes 9:10
Whatever your hand finds to do, do it with all your might, for in the grave, where you are going, there is neither working nor planning nor knowledge nor wisdom.

1 Corinthians 15:58
Therefore, my dear brothers, stand firm. Let nothing move you. Always give yourselves fully to the work of the Lord, because you know that your labor in the Lord is not in vain.

Hebrews 6:10-11

God is not unjust; he will not forget your work and the love you have shown him as you have helped his people and continue to help them. We want each of you to show this same diligence to the very end, in order to make your hope sure.

Colossians 3:23-24

Whatever you do, work at it with all your heart, as working for the Lord, not for men, since you know that you will receive an inheritance from the Lord as a reward. It is the Lord Christ you are serving.

Ecclesiastes 3:9-13

What does the worker gain from his toil? I have seen the burden God has laid on men. He has made everything beautiful in its time. He has also set eternity in the hearts of men; yet they cannot fathom what God has done from beginning to end. I know that there is nothing better for men than to be happy and do good while they live. That everyone may eat and drink, and find satisfaction in all his toil—this is the gift of God.

OBSCENITY

Words that are spoken,
    when one's spirit is broken.
Terms that are used
    when one wants to abuse.
Slang with a hidden undertone,
    a double meaning for something wrong.
Phrases without a purpose
    that are simply useless.
Close your ears and cover your eyes,
    protect your relationship with the Father on
    High.

Quick Script: Matthew 12:37

For by your words you will be acquitted, and
by your words you will be condemned.

WORDS THAT WOUND

From the mouths of everyone, from young children to
seniors, spew words that wound our hearts and ears

with sharp-edged arrows.

For the young, we wonder where they heard that type of language, because we don't say those words in our house. But they attend school, overhear conversations, read graffiti, listen to the radio, and look at television. They're young and can be taught what is appropriate and what is not. So we are concerned, understand, realize that they might not know better, and then try to instruct them —raising them up right as God commands.

The teenagers may be going through a phase or trying to impress a group. We correct them and hold our breaths waiting for them to move on to the next phase in their development.

But what about the adults—the people in the company cafeteria, the executives in the boardroom, the group talking around the coffee pot, and the worker who just made a mistake—what excuse can we attach to their verbal attacks, insults, and disrespect? We are tired of their offensive language. It should not be used in a professional environment; there is no place for it in the workplace or any other place for that matter. It not only bothers us, but it disturbs others, especially when the offensive language is targeted at them.

As Christians, we can take some action with God on our side. First, we must pray about the situation and let the Holy Spirit lead us in the best way to approach the situation. We may need to tell the person who is talking that the language he is using is offensive and inappropriate for the office. Or we might want to monitor a friend for a day and make a note of how many times she used the Lord's name in vain or cursed. When we present that information, she may be surprised.

By all means, we don't need to stand around and listen to what's said. We can excuse ourselves and leave. Hopefully a few of them will get the message. Certainly there are a number of actions we can take to reduce the obscenity floating through the air, pricking our ears and heart.

However, our challenge may be even greater. We may be the ones who will get people to change their language, at least in the office. If we feel the Lord's leading, we might need to go on a mission to clean up the office. If we proceed prayerfully, the change will overtake individuals' entire lives. Everyone can benefit from fewer wounding words.

———————

Throwing Out the Garbage: Get rid of the obscenity in and around you—the same way you take out the trash at home so it can be picked up, taken away, and incinerated. This is trash that does not require recycling.

———————

Dear Father, cleanse my mouth and tighten my lips so I won't join in or respond to words that are offensive to You and to others. Let me set an example for others. I pray for the courage to speak up instead of running away when wrong things are said. Amen.

OVERPOWERING OBSCENITY

- Instead of going along with the crowd, set an example by demonstrating the proper way to talk.

- Wrong words can weaken the spirit and truth God has given.

- Obscenity places a wedge between you and friends and family, coworkers, and Christ.

- Every time you use obscenity, think of it as a painful noise to God's ears. Don't give Him an earache or an earful.

- Denounce the use of obscenity in your presence. It's okay for people to feel uncomfortable saying those words around you and maybe they will stop saying them around others.

- Let your words be better than silence; otherwise say nothing.

- Don't accept obscenity in any form, written or verbal.

- Check your vocabulary, including those words that you substitute for profanity. Get rid of anything that is questionable.

- You can't correct others when you occasionally slip and do the same thing.

- Challenge your coworkers to a day of not cursing.

- Acknowledge and praise your coworkers when they curtail or discontinue their foul language. Thank them for respecting you and ultimately themselves and others.

- Pray for a clean heart along with a clean mouth so more people will want to hear what you say.

- We may face obstacles in our efforts, but we are in a world that needs to hear the proper Word.

Heavenly Father, I pray that I set a good example for someone today through my conversation. Lord, I thank You for giving me the opportunity to show others how You have changed my life and how theirs can be changed also. Please continue to guide me for I know I can't do this alone. Amen.

———————

SCRIPTURE REFERENCES

Ephesians 5:3-4
But among you there must not be even a hint of sexual immorality, or of any kind of impurity, or of greed, because these are improper for God's holy people. Nor should there be obscenity, foolish talk or coarse joking, which are out of place, but rather thanksgiving.

Proverbs 4:24
Put away perversity from your mouth; keep corrupt talk far from your lips.

Proverbs 6:12,15
A scoundrel and villain, who goes about with a corrupt mouth, . . . Therefore disaster will

overtake him in an instant; he will suddenly be
destroyed—without remedy.

Jude 10
Yet these men speak abusively against whatever
they do not understand; and what things they
do understand by instinct, like unreasoning
animals—these are the very things that destroy
them.

Job 15:5-6
Your sin prompts your mouth; you adopt the
tongue of the crafty. Your own mouth condemns
you, not mine; your own lips testify against you.

Psalm 94:3-5
How long will the wicked, O Lord, how long
will the wicked be jubilant? They pour out
arrogant words; all the evildoers are full of
boasting. They crush your people, O Lord; they
oppress your inheritance.

Psalm 39:1
I said, "I will watch my ways and keep my tongue
from sin; I will put a muzzle on my mouth. . . . "

Colossians 4:6
Let your conversation be always full of grace,
seasoned with salt, so that you may know how
to answer everyone.

PATIENCE

She said she'd be late.
She was having trouble with her car,
    but you haven't heard any more so far.
You tap your feet and fingers,
    then you begin to make calls.
Next, you start pacing the halls.
She's more than a little late.
When she finally strolls in
    she acts as if she doesn't know when workdays
        begin.
Off comes the coat, hat, and boots.
Instead of sitting down,
    she begins to make the round.
You've had enough and you're ready to burst.
As you approach, you hear what she is saying,
    but your mouth is already in motion, with
        anger spraying.
Her excuse was legitimate.
As the voices in the room hush,
    your lack of trust makes you blush.
You were too impatient to wait for the truth.
Now you have no choice but to apologize,
    especially since you realize that once again you
        let your emotions rule your heart
            and cloud your eyes,
                driven by the selfish ways you despise.

The end of a matter is better than its beginning, and patience is better than pride.

I Want It Now!

We deal with the impatient, unreasonable demands of "I needed it yesterday. I want it ASAP! When will you be finished? How long will it take? I can't wait" every day at work, whether it's our boss, a coworker, or someone to whom we are providing a service. What happens when we rush? Accidents and mistakes. The undue pressure makes us nervous and insecure. It may even make us angry; we may feel as though we want to punish the person pressuring us by doing less than our best.

Guard yourself from letting someone else's impatience put you in a retaliatory or compromising position. God demands that we do our best, that we do not compromise ourselves against His Word—and remember that we are equal to everyone else He created.

God is not only patient with us, but He is patient with those who are impatient. He can use us to set an example if we refuse to respond negatively to the situation. Our example will be like a familiar saying, "Kill them with kindness," but in this case we should change it to " Save them with kindness." We can take pleasure in having that impatient person wonder why we keep smiling, why we don't get upset, why we don't argue, and why we say thank you. Maybe the impatient people will come to realize that they need the same Friend that keeps us peaceful and joyous.

Even more important, we must be careful to control our own impatience. As Christians, we are not immune to this emotion. It comes from wanting our own way, *now.* We need to be careful to wait on God, accepting whatever He sends when He sends it, rather than trying to force people and events to fit our own timetable. When impatient words spring to our lips, we must discipline ourselves to control them, for our impatience will negate Christ's witness of love in our lives.

God does all things well. When we truly believe that, we will cease to feel impatient.

———————

Rushing by Your Blessings: Sometimes we move so fast that we don't allow God time to do His work in our lives. We interrupt, dismiss, and demand, disturbing God's well-timed plan. As you go about your day, take the time to wait on God. He will give you His answer in His time.

Most mighty Father in heaven, I ask You to give me a willing spirit of patience even when it seems as if things are not going how I think they should. Keep me focused on what You want for me. Let me remain focused on doing what is before me until You order my next step. Amen.

———————

WAITING TO WAIT

- We can never sacrifice too much in the light of all that Christ sacrificed for us.

- Do not be tired, impatient, or weary when waiting on the Lord.

- Concentrate on what the Lord wants you to do right now, not what you think He wants you to do later.

- Serving the Lord requires commitment to His plan and timing; remember we are not in this alone.

- If it comes too easy and too fast, it may be useless. Most good things are worth the wait.

- When things are done quickly and hastily, they are usually not done correctly.

- When pressured to make decisions, usually the choice is wrong.

- All things take time to mature, including the work that God plans for you at your place of employment.

- The Lord has been patient with us; we have to be equally as patient with Him and others.

- Waiting requires total surrender and submission as a servant.

- God works with us at different paces, so you can't expect everyone to be at the same point.

- Don't rush into what God doesn't want you to be involved in yet.

- God gives you just what He wants you to have, when He wants you to have it, then He waits patiently to be able to give you more. Deal with what He has given you so He can be free to fill you up.

Almighty God of grace, give me the wisdom and patience to accept whatever is going on around me. You know what these things are and You are allowing them to happen for a reason. I am thankful to be able to look beyond current circumstances, realizing that You have a purpose and place for me. Amen.

————

SCRIPTURE REFERENCES

2 Peter 3:9
The Lord is not slow in keeping his promise, as some understand slowness. He is patient with you, not wanting anyone to perish, but everyone to come to repentance.

Proverbs 14:29
A patient man has great understanding, but a quick-tempered man displays folly.

Proverbs 15:18
A hot-tempered man stirs up dissension, but a patient man calms a quarrel.

Proverbs 19:11

A man's wisdom gives him patience; it is to his glory to overlook an offense.

Proverbs 16:32

Better a patient man than a warrior, a man who controls his temper than one who takes a city.

Proverbs 25:15

Through patience a ruler can be persuaded, and a gentle tongue can break a bone.

2 Peter 3:15

Bear in mind that our Lord's patience means salvation, just as our dear brother Paul also wrote you with the wisdom that God gave him.

2 Corinthians 6:4-6

Rather, as servants of God we commend ourselves in every way: in great endurance; in troubles, hardships and distresses; in beatings, imprisonments, and riots; in hard work, sleepless nights and hunger; in purity, understanding, patience and kindness; in the Holy Spirit and in sincere love.

Galatians 5:22-23

But the fruit of the Spirit is love, joy, peace, patience, kindness, goodness, faithfulness, gentleness and self-control. Against such things there is no law.

Colossians 3:12

Therefore, as God's chosen people, holy and dearly loved, clothe yourselves with compassion, kindness, humility, gentleness and patience.

Romans 12:12

Be joyful in hope, patient in affliction, faithful in prayer.

John 15:4-5

Remain in me, and I will remain in you. No branch can bear fruit by itself; it must remain in the vine. Neither can you bear fruit unless you remain in me. "I am the vine; you are the branches. If a man remains in me and I in him, he will bear much fruit; apart from me you can do nothing.

PERFORMANCE REVIEWS

You go beyond what's required,
    and never say that you're tired.
You arrive early and stay late,
    anticipating how you'll rate.
You've come up with objections
    to the anticipated rejections.
You've done the best you can,
    unfair criticism you just can't understand.
Remember, he is just a man
    unable to judge another or take a stand.
Sure, he'll have a say
    but respond in a faithful way.
Don't let the words of today
    interfere with the real judgment day.

Quick Script: James 1:12

Blessed is the man who perseveres under trial,
because when he has stood the test, he will
receive the crown of life that God has
promised to those who love him.

Measures, Benchmarks, and Yardsticks

We are constantly trying to compare what we've done to what someone or something indicates we should have done. No matter how much we do or how hard we try, we never seem to reach the top pinnacle of achievement. It seems that the closer we get to it, the more it moves away, always just a little beyond our reach. And if we think "we've made it," we find that we want more, or it wasn't what we expected.

These self-imposed measures of success and status are what keeps some of us driving ahead like a runaway bulldozer. Eventually, we run out of gas—or crash—if we don't get on the right road. The road that God has paved.

Even when we were originally on the right road, those external reviews of our progress, productivity, and job knowledge can really take us on a detour. We act as if our performance review was the only thing that mattered. We can save ourselves many heartaches and headaches by realizing that achievement, power, fame, knowledge, and money do not bring peace, joy, and eternal life.

We all hate criticism. But when we are secure in Christ's salvation, no longer needing to prove ourselves, then we are free to learn from these reviews of our performance. None of us is perfect; we all have room to grow, and performance reviews can help us see where we need to concentrate our efforts to change.

As Christians, we should always do the very best we can. As long as we are performing as Christ wants us to, then we can be confident of His review of our performance—even if our supervisor thinks otherwise.

A Song and a Dance: Are you tap dancing, singing a song to a tune other than the gospel's? Are you off God's key because you had to compromise the Word to stay in step? If you are not producing melodies and joyous sounds for the Lord, you need to turn the page and change your tune real soon. Turning the page may take a drastic change in your life, but as long as the change is in concert with God's Word, have faith that He will show you the next note to strike. Let God's will play on!

Morning Prayer

Most honorable Father, I praise Your name this morning as I revel in the knowledge that only You are my judge. I accept the responsibility to do the work You have prepared for me and will show respect for the person You have placed to guide me. Above all, I pray for help in remaining focused on doing Your work, considering always how You will view my actions. Amen.

RENEWED BY THE REVIEW

• No one will ever get a perfect review. They simply are not designed to list all of our wonderful attributes. Remember that your supervisor is almost obligated to find at least one thing to say about you that needs improvement. Anyway, since none of us are perfect, why should we expect a perfect review?

• Use the burden of failure and criticism to build you spiritually.

• If you don't want to fail, stop trying so hard to please, accepting the judgment of everyone except God.

• Don't let monetary promises and rewards possess your thoughts and actions.

• To know God's strengths, you must know your weaknesses.

• When receiving constructive criticism, think of all you stand to gain. Listen and act with obedience.

• Remember that a review is what has happened in the past. Leave it there and move on.

• Worry ends where your faith begins.

- Your performance review is of only a small part of your life and as such should be viewed that way. The larger part is your relationship with God.

- When you are giving a review, focus on how to help the person from a positive standpoint rather than simply pointing out the areas that are lacking.

- If you want a good performance review from the One who counts, discipline yourself in reading the Bible, praying, forgiving, and rejecting sinful thoughts and actions.

Evening Prayer

Almighty God, I offer my total life as You see it for inspection and correction so that I may righteously enjoy all that You have given and promised to me on earth and in heaven. I ask for listening ears and seeing eyes to do as You desire. Take away my defensive attitude. Make me open to criticism, willing to change. Remind me always that my only worth comes from You, and that Your grace is free, regardless of my success or failure. Amen.

SCRIPTURE REFERENCES

Psalm 7:10-11

My shield is God Most High, who saves the upright in heart. God is a righteous judge, a God who expresses his wrath every day.

Colossians 3:23-24

Whatever you do, work at it with all your heart, as working for the Lord, not for men, since you know that you will receive an inheritance from the Lord as a reward. It is the Lord Christ you are serving.

Proverbs 14:23

All hard work brings a profit, but mere talk leads only to poverty.

Ecclesiastes 3:15

Whatever is has already been, and what will be has been before; and God will call the past to account.

1 Corinthians 3:12-17

If any man builds on this foundation using gold, silver, costly stones, wood, hay, or straw, his work will be shown for what it is, because the Day will bring it to light. It will be revealed with fire, and the fire will test the quality of each man's work. If what he has built survives, he will receive his reward. If it is burned up, he will suffer loss; he himself will be saved, but only as one escaping through the flames. Don't you know that you yourselves are God's temple and that God's Spirit lives in you? If anyone destroys God's temple, God will destroy him; for God's temple is sacred, and you are that temple.

2 Chronicles 19:6-7

He told them, "Consider carefully what you do, because you are not judging for man but for the Lord, who is with you whenever you give a verdict. Now let the fear of the Lord be upon you. Judge carefully, for with the Lord our God there is no injustice or partiality or bribery."

Romans 2:1-4

You, therefore, have no excuse, you who pass judgment on someone else, for at whatever point you judge the other, you are condemning yourself, because you who pass judgment do the same things. Now we know that God's judgment against those who do such things is based on truth. So when you, a mere man, pass judgment on them and yet do the same things, do you think you will escape God's judgment? Or do you show contempt for the riches of his kindness, tolerance and patience, not realizing that God's kindness leads you towards repentance?

Hebrews 12:11

No discipline seems pleasant at the time, but painful. Later on, however, it produces a harvest of righteousness and peace for those who have been trained by it.

Ecclesiastes 5:19-20

Moreover, when God gives any man wealth and possessions, and enables him to enjoy them, to accept his lot and be happy in his work—this is a gift of God. He seldom reflects on the days of his life, because God keeps him occupied with gladness of heart.

2 Corinthians 9:13

Because of the service by which you have proved yourselves, men will praise God for the obedience that accompanies your confession of the gospel of Christ, and for your generosity in sharing with them and with everyone else.

PRIDE

We try to keep it inside,
     but it's something we can't hide,
      it's our foolish pride.
Who are we to stake claim
     to what we don't own,
      to get credit for what God has shown.
Through our minds and our hands,
He empowers all our plans.
Give God the credit and glory,
     for the success story,
      and the contract signed,
       according to His deadline.
Correct people when they give you the praise,
     tell them it's God's hand they should clasp and
      raise.
When they place you on the throne,
     let them know that you've done nothing alone.
Through Him, He makes a way
     for our triumphs every day.

Quick Script: Proverbs 29:23

A man's pride brings him low, but a man of
lowly spirit gains honor.

Pride Is a Thorn in Your Side

How can having pride be a thorn in your side? That just doesn't seem to make sense when we have always been told to do everything with pride and to do our very best.

Our parents want to be proud of us. We strive for the best grades so we can graduate at the top of the class. Having our name printed in the newspaper for a job promotion is what we want and what the company expects.

In fact, the promotions and new hire page is one of the first sections many people turn to when reading the newspaper. We look to see who we know, count the number of people listed from our own company, and see who has been promoted from our current job level to one that is higher. Maybe it's time to demand a promotion. After all, those other people who were promoted have less experience and were in their positions less time. Their promotion makes us look like we aren't on the fast track and that we may have reached our top or the glass ceiling with this company. Maybe it's time to start looking for a job with another company where the management will appreciate our abilities. In goes that prickly thorn. Until we find a better situation, the thorn seems to grow, turn, get deeper, and even becomes sharper. It hurts us and hurts others.

We have mistakenly placed pride as a measure of our worth among our family, coworkers, and friends. Even worse, we have put ourselves in a position of being judged by man and what man values instead of the judgment of God. We've also taken claim for things we don't own and lifted them up to people like an offering for approval and acceptance. Our pride has taken us out of the favorable presence of God and because of that we will never be happy.

It's time for us to remove the thorn of pride and replace it with the burning desire to please God. Knowing that God is proud of us is the best "pride" for which we can strive.

———

Getting Rid of Pride: Sometimes when you look at a word, you see another contained within the word. In this case, you can see the word *rid* right in the middle of the word p*rid*e. Maybe you've never noticed it before. However, when you see it, you see it for a reason. God may be showing it to you to make a point. If your pride springs from anything other than Christ's saving work in your life, then it's probably time you thought about getting rid of your pride.

———

Dear God, my Father, I thank You for giving me another day to perform the work You have set for me. I accept the work gladly and willfully, knowing that whatever it may be, it is for You and Your Glory. I pray that others will see You at work through my work and realize that it is only with You that I can accomplish anything. I give all honor, praise, and glory to You. Amen.

————————

NOT BY MY WORKS

- As you fill with pride, your faith in God deflates. Remember that all things are made possible by God who works through you.

- No one wants to be around someone who is always patting himself on the back.

- Pride may build you up, but it will ultimately let you down.

- Avoid drawing self-centered attention to your work; God wants you to have the right motive for doing His work.

- When was the last time you admitted that you were wrong? Willingness to admit that you are wrong allows room for growth and learning. Admit when you are wrong, and keep quiet about being right.

- Protecting yourself when you are wrong does not allow for correction or resolution.

- God gives us the opportunity to earn what we need and sometimes what we want, but we must remember that this is available through God, not ourselves or anyone else. Taking the praise for work is stealing the glory from God.

- What is your first motive in the things you do? Is it to receive praise and recognition—or to please God?

Evening Prayer

Most honorable Father, I recognize that I neglected to give You the credit for what You enabled me to accomplish today. I ask for forgiveness and for another chance to show my coworkers and others how You enable me (and can enable them) to do the seemingly impossible while meeting the challenges of the workday. Amen.

SCRIPTURE REFERENCES

Proverbs 11:2
When pride comes, then comes disgrace, but with humility comes wisdom.

James 1:9-10
The brother in humble circumstances ought to take pride in his high position. But the one who is rich should take pride in his low position, because he will pass away like a wild flower.

Proverbs 16:18-19
Pride goes before destruction, a haughty spirit before a fall. Better to be lowly in spirit and among the oppressed than to share plunder with the proud.

Proverbs 8:13
To fear the Lord is to hate evil; I hate pride and arrogance, evil behavior and perverse speech.

Psalm 56:2
My slanderers pursue me all day long; many are attacking me in their pride.

Leviticus 26:19-20
I will break down your stubborn pride and make the sky above you like iron and the ground beneath you like bronze. Your strength will be spent in vain, because your soil will not

yield its crops, nor will the trees of the land yield their fruit.

Psalm 31:18
Let their lying lips be silenced, for with pride and contempt they speak arrogantly against the righteous.

Isaiah 25:11-12
. . .God will bring down their pride despite the cleverness of their hands. He will bring down your high fortified walls and lay them low; he will bring them down to the ground, to the very dust.

Ezekiel 7:24-25
I will bring the most wicked of the nations to take possession of their houses; I will put an end to the pride of the mighty, and their sanctuaries will be desecrated. When terror comes, they will seek peace, but there will be none.

2 Corinthians 5:12-15
We are not trying to commend ourselves to you again, but are giving you an opportunity to take pride in us, so that you can answer those who take pride in what is seen rather than in what is in the heart. If we are out of our mind, it is for the sake of God; if we are in our right mind, it is for you. For Christ's love compels us, because we are convinced that one died for all,

and therefore all died. And he died for all, that those who live should no longer live for themselves but for him who died for them and was raised again.

Ecclesiastes 7:8

The end of a matter is better than its beginning, and patience is better than pride.

SALARIES AND RAISES

You're not getting paid enough for what you do.
You're missing money that you're really due.
If you have to work for less,
    just don't do your best.
If you've reached the top of the scale,
    it's time to consider the word curtail.
If they can't pay beyond the top,
    let the work stop.
Maybe this is how you feel
    about your financial deal.
But don't be contrary
    about what is monetary.
You may think there's disparity,
    but you really need some clarity.
Money can't measure
    that you're God's treasure.
It's just a distraction
    a source of dissatisfaction.
A salary, a bonus, or a raise
    means nothing until you give God the praise.
Your real pay
    will come on judgment day.
Only then will you receive the gifts and glory,
    promised in the Bible's story.

———————

No one can serve two masters. Either he will hate the one and love the other, or he will be devoted to the one and despise the other. You cannot serve both God and Money.

DIALING FOR DOLLARS

There used to be a game show called "Dialing for Dollars." Depending upon what numbers were dialed (this was before touch-tone telephones), you could win money. Faithfully, people would watch the program and pray that their telephone number would be dialed. They would stop everything, change the course of their day, sit by the telephone, and wait for their telephone number to be dialed. Then if their prayers were answered, they would pick up the ringing telephone and instantly become worth something.

Money gives us a sense of worth, power, acceptance, and importance. We are jealous when someone we know makes more than we do; we dream about what we would do with more money. We make plans, just in case we get that raise we're hoping for. If we don't get it, we begin to think more about what we don't have rather than what we do, and disappointment develops, growing deeper, destroying our ability to be satisfied.

Satisfaction in any situation comes from only one source and it is not money. Satisfaction comes from knowing that God is the ultimate provider, whether in the form of money, food, shelter, safety, employment, or love.

What number are you dialing? Are you calling the personnel department and your boss? Are you leaving messages for the union leader? Are you rewriting your contract? Or are you calling upon God to provide for your needs? Use your direct line to God. You'll never get a busy signal and you'll always get a response. Don't get hung up on powerless lines. Remember to make the right connection.

———————

Every Day Is Pay Day: We don't have to wait until Friday to get paid and count our money. We are paid every day we are alive. We are paid with a new life in Christ today and the promise of eternal life. We may not remember how we've been paid in the past or know how we will be paid in the future. The one thing we can count on, though, is that God provides for us every day.

———————

Dear Father in heaven, the Almighty One, I pray that I will never take for granted all that You have done for me and given to me. I ask for the insight to know that You are my provider and that I should never place the value of earthly, human rewards over the provisions You have made for me. I pray for patience and gratitude and full faith in You. Amen.

BANK ON CHRIST

- Your employer is not the true source of your money. God is the source. He supplies all that you need through various means.

- True wealth is not contingent upon raises and bonuses. Stay focused on permanent not temporary wealth. Give thanks for the abundance and prosperity of life on all levels, not just those that are monetary.

- Don't center your trust or security in money rather than God. Don't let monetary promises and rewards possess your thoughts and actions.

- Focus on managing the resources God has already invested in and through you. Have you maximized your resources?

- Are you willing to serve God without a guaranteed salary increase? God will try you with a little to determine what you would do if He gave you a lot.

- Money is a slave master that will always whip you in the end. You will never win.

- When you follow the standards of salary ranges and net worth, you will never have enough. When you follow God, you will see your true worth and wealth.

- Money can't buy happiness, love, and peace.

- Once you start measuring everything by how much money you make, you might not be able to stop. Don't let the love of money give you a sense of false happiness.

- Wealth can isolate you from reality, affecting your values and derailing you from God's plan for your life.

Dear God, salaries are so uncertain in today's working world. You know how preoccupied I can be about money. Forgive me for spending time worrying instead of praising You. I am so thankful that regardless of how much money I make, I will be okay and my family will be fine. I am grateful for the knowledge and assurance that You will provide for our needs regardless of what things may look like on the surface. I pray that I can convey this same sense of security to those around me. Use me, Father, to ease others' worry; help me to point their eyes to You. Amen.

SCRIPTURE REFERENCES

Isaiah 52:3
For this is what the Lord says: "You were sold for nothing, and without money you will be redeemed."

Acts 8:20-22
Peter answered: "May your money perish with you, because you thought you could buy the

gift of God with money! You have no part or share in this ministry, because your heart is not right before God. Repent of this wickedness and pray to the Lord. Perhaps he will forgive you for having such a thought in your heart.

1 Timothy 6:7-10

For we brought nothing into the world, and we can take nothing out of it. But if we have food and clothing, we will be content with that. People who want to get rich fall into temptation and a trap and into many foolish and harmful desires that plunge men into ruin and destruction. For the love of money is a root of all kinds of evil. Some people, eager for money, have wandered from the faith and pierced themselves with many griefs.

Proverbs 17:16

Of what use is money in the hand of a fool, since he has no desire to get wisdom?

Ecclesiastes 10:6

Fools are put in many high positions, while the rich occupy the low ones.

Matthew 6:19-21

Do not store up for yourselves treasures on earth, where moth and rust destroy, and where thieves break in and steal. But store up for yourselves treasures in heaven, where moth and rust do not destroy, and where thieves do not break in and steal. For where your treasure is, there your heart will be also.

Luke 16:10-11

Whoever can be trusted with very little can also be trusted with much, and whoever is dishonest with very little will also be dishonest with much. So if you have not been trustworthy in handling worldly wealth, who will trust you with true riches?

James 4:13-15

Now listen, you who say, "Today or tomorrow we will go to this or that city, spend a year there, carry on business and make money." Why, you do not even know what will happen tomorrow. What is your life? You are a mist that appears for a little while and then vanishes. Instead, you ought to say, "If it is the Lord's will, we will live and do this or that."

James 5:1-5

Now listen, you rich people, weep and wail because of the misery that is coming upon you. Your wealth has rotted, and moths have eaten your clothes. Your gold and silver are corroded. Their corrosion will testify against you and eat your flesh like fire. You have hoarded wealth in

the last days. Look! The wages you failed to pay
the workmen who mowed your fields are crying
out against you. The cries of the harvesters have
reached the ears of the Lord Almighty. You have
lived on earth in luxury and self-indulgence. You
have fattened yourselves in the day of slaughter.

Ecclesiastes 5:10-11

Whoever loves money never has money
enough; whoever loves wealth is never satisfied with his income. This too is meaningless.
As goods increase, so do those who consume
them. And what benefit are they to the owner
except to feast his eyes on them?

SELFISHNESS

When we take our money and hold tight
    concentrating on it with all our might,
We act as though it belongs only to us.
That shows our lack of trust,
    for if we really care,
        then we will share.
Knowledge and wealth must be released
    for God's kingdom to increase.
If our goal is to reach,
    then we must not hoard but teach.
How can we influence and enlist,
    if we don't assist?
We must freely give
    in order to fully live.
The more we try to possess,
    the more we end up with less.
God has entrusted us with His way,
    expecting us to share it every day.
Wherever we go and whatever we do,
    to His word we must remain true.

Quick Script: Romans 2:8
But for those who are self-seeking and who
reject the truth and follow evil, there will be
wrath and anger.

YOURS, MINE, AND OURS

When we were little children, our parents constantly reminded us to share our toys with others. We would say "mine" and hold the toy tight, until our parents pried it out of our hands. These were our first lessons against selfishness.

As older children, we promised our best friends that we'd share everything we have with each other. "Share and share alike" is what we said. We exchanged clothes, comic books, and sometimes even our homework assignments. When one of us couldn't come out and play until our work was done, we'd pitch in and help the other so we could move on to the important tasks of building tree houses and making mud pies.

Life was so much simpler then. Since those days, somehow selfishness has crept into our lives. We've forgotten the pleasure of doing things together, sharing our knowledge with others, the joy of working together. We've stopped focusing on "we" and instead begin everything with "me." We like to think of ourselves as self-sufficient superheroes. We can do everything ourselves, we don't need help, and we know it all.

Why should we help others when we've worked so hard to get where we are? If we share our knowledge, then others will get credit for what we know. If we had to work hard, they should, too. That's the attitude that all too many of us have.

The truth is, selfishness has its roots back in our childhood, back when we started competing for top honors at school or when we didn't want to let our brother have some of our Halloween candy. Now, since we've moved into the professional world, selfishness separates us from others. We covet knowledge and possessions; we refuse to share, just like we did back when we were toddlers, except now there's no one to tell us our attitude is unjustified. Competitiveness and the desire for recognition create a selfish and insecure nature, especially in the work environment.

We are to give as God has given to us. We are to serve others as God serves us. We are to give God the recognition for His work and for everything that He has created and enabled us to create. We cannot claim or hoard what is not rightfully ours. Would we want God to be selfish toward us, holding back His blessings? Do we want God to separate Himself from us because He cannot trust us with the knowledge He shares?

Selfish and Alone: If you like being alone, try being selfish. It's a proven way of keeping everyone away, including God. God did not give His Son for you only. His spirit of giving is what He expects of each of us, even if it means helping a coworker advance. The more you give, the more room you have to receive. If you are so bottled up with all the things you insist on keeping, you will never have room to grow nor will there be enough space for anyone else.

Almighty Father, I give all thanks and glory to You for all the things that You have done, not just for me but for the entire world. I pray for an increase in my spirit of giving and sharing and that it will come naturally, without any hesitation or reservation. Let me take delight in sharing as much as I can with others. Amen.

SELFISHNESS STUNTS GROWTH

- Are you a spiritual toddler, holding on to everything and thinking that it is yours exclusively?

- Do you volunteer information readily, or wait until you are asked? Do you take delight in having people have to ask you for information? Do you hold back just a little of what you know to keep the person coming back to you for more?

- If you are trying to have more than others, expect less from God.

- God looks at the heart, not worldly possessions. God is pleased when you make a conscious effort to be more like Him by sharing with others.

- Do you have a giving heart, mind, mouth, and spirit? Or, are you still clamping your mouth, turning your head, closing your eyes, and idling your hands?

- When you give, do you expect something in return?

- Are you looking out for your own interests—or are you concerned about advancing the Kingdom of God?

- The more you serve God, the less you will serve yourself, and the more you will serve others. Try thinking less of yourself and more of God.

- Your self-serving efforts to look good among others are always exposed to God.

- Whatever you keep for yourself, God can easily take away. There is nothing you can hide from God, including your selfishness.

Almighty God, I admit my weakness in sharing all of the wonderful things You have provided to me. I recognize that I attempt to gain favor by using what You have given to my advantage. I pray that this bondage to selfishness will be removed from my soul and replaced with the freedom and joy of giving. Let me no longer think about myself first, second, or third—only last, if at all. Amen.

SCRIPTURE REFERENCES

Philippians 2:3-5
Do nothing out of selfish ambition or vain conceit, but in humility consider others better than yourselves. Each of you should look not only to your own interests, but also to the interests of others. Your attitude should be the same as that of Christ Jesus.

Matthew 23:5-12
Everything they do is done for men to see: They make their phylacteries wide and the tassels on their garments long; they love the place of honor

at banquets and the most important seats in the synagogues; they love to be greeted in the marketplaces and to have men call them "Rabbi." But you are not to be called "Rabbi," for you have only one Master and you are all brothers. And do not call anyone on earth "father," for you have one Father, and he is in heaven. Nor are you to be called "teacher," for you have one Teacher, the Christ. The greatest among you will be your servant. For whoever exalts himself will be humbled, and whoever humbles himself will be exalted.

Romans 7:7-9

What shall we say, then? Is the law sin? Certainly not! Indeed I would not have known what sin was except through the law. For I would not have known what coveting really was if the law had not said, "Do not covet." But sin, seizing the opportunity afforded by the commandment, produced in me every kind of covetous desire. For apart from law, sin is dead. Once I was alive apart from law; but when the commandment came, sin sprang to life and I died.

Matthew 23:13-14

Woe to you, teachers of the law and Pharisees, you hypocrites! You shut the kingdom of heaven in men's faces. You yourselves do not enter, nor will you let those enter who are trying to.

Acts 20:32-38

Now I commit you to God and to the word of his grace, which can build you up and give you an inheritance among all those who are sanctified. I have not coveted anyone's silver or gold or clothing. You yourselves know that these hands of mine have supplied my own needs and the needs of my companions. In everything I did, I showed you that by this kind of hard work we must help the weak, remembering the words the Lord Jesus himself said: "It is more blessed to give than to receive."

Psalm 119:36

Turn my heart toward your statutes and not toward selfish gain.

John 3:30

He must become greater; I must become less.

Proverbs 18:1

An unfriendly man pursues selfish ends; he defies all sound judgment.

Galatians 6:9-10

Let us not become weary in doing good, for at the proper time we will reap a harvest if we do not give up. Therefore, as we have opportunity, let us do good to all people, especially to those who belong to the family of believers.

James 3:13-16

Who is wise and understanding among you? Let him show it by his good life, by deeds done in the humility that comes from wisdom. But if you harbor bitter envy and selfish ambition in your hearts, do not boast about it or deny the truth. Such "wisdom" does not come down from heaven but is earthly, unspiritual, of the devil. For where you have envy and selfish ambition, there you find disorder and every evil practice.

Matthew 23:25

Woe to you, teachers of the law and Pharisees, you hypocrites! You clean the outside of the cup and dish, but inside they are full of greed and self-indulgence.

Sexual Immorality

It's in their magazines and books
    and they try to get you to look.
You try to keep your distance
    thinking this is a form of resistance.
But you can't close your ears
    to the indecent lewdness you hear.
It's no laughing matter
    nor is it idle chatter.
The subject of the conversation
    is full of degradation.
You really want to criticize
    but you fear that your job will be jeopardized.
So you continue to run and turn away
    not taking action according to God's way.
You just didn't think about it much
    until the day you were touched.
Now you've become the object
    of their indecent, sexual subject.
It can happen to another
    so you can't let it go further.
Who knows who's next,
    as they cheapen the act of sex.
What happened is not your fault
    but you'll jeopardize others if they aren't
        caught.
Call on God to help you end
    something sinful that should have never been.

What goes into a man's mouth does not make him "unclean," but what comes out of his mouth, that is what makes him "unclean."

OBSESSION AND PASSION FOR JESUS

We get obsessed and develop passions for many things, and some of them are the wrong things. Our passion should be for God and His Word. When we displace our spiritual passion with unhealthy obsessions, then we jeopardize our relationship both with God and with friends and loved ones.

Sexual immorality can begin so gradually that we barely notice. We may begin by entertaining more and more sexual thoughts about our coworkers. We excuse ourselves, however, telling ourselves there's no harm in just *thinking*. We forget that God looks on the heart. Christ said that the person who looks on another with lust is just as guilty as the one who commits adultery. God asks us to be as pure on the inside as we act on the outside. Otherwise, we're simply hypocrites.

We may find next that we enjoy telling stories with sexual innuendoes that are disrespectful and crude. We're not hurting anyone, we tell ourselves; surely there's no harm in a little joke. But we fail to recognize that our words have power, and we must be careful to use them for good rather than evil.

Soon, our stories may progress to sexual teasing and flirting. It's all innocent, we convince ourselves; but if we were honest, our hearts would tell us otherwise. It's all good fun, to make remarks and laugh with the others, forgetting that not everyone is laughing. The victims of our disrespect may hide their hurt, but it's real nevertheless.

We may not realize the spiraling effort of our sexual immorality until one of our children gets in trouble at school for doing the same thing we do and laugh about. Or maybe our daughter comes home and tells us what was said to her as she worked during her summer internship; we're angry at first—and then we realize we've said the same words to a coworker. When the words turn into actions directed at our spouse, we're incensed. We'd never go that far, we tell ourselves—and yet sexual assault is the natural end to the progression of sexual immorality.

Sex is one of God's sacred gifts to humanity. When we cheapen it with our thoughts and words and actions, then in effect we are spitting on God's gift. We are taking something that was intended for love and life, and using it as a joke, a joke that can hurt and even lead to physical harm. The reality of this becomes obvious once one of our own is victimized by sexual immorality.

We hear more and more about sexual harassment on the job and at colleges. But this type of behavior is everywhere and should not be acceptable anywhere. What may start as a joke may infiltrate our homes and even our churches. We must examine everything that we do, say, read, and think for the smallest speck of sexual immorality. Think about the songs we listen to on the radio, the movies we see, the magazines we read, the television programs we watch, the comedians we listen to, and almost every contact we have with others. Do you think Jesus would have done the same things? Who are you patterning your life after, Jesus or your buddies?

Our passion should be for Jesus, for only He can wipe us clean from unhealthy obsession.

From the Mouths of Babes: Is there anything worse than hearing a teenager use sexually explicit language? Yes. What's worse is that they got it from you or some other adult. Babies learn how to talk by emulating what we say. As they grow, they emulate our actions, too, trying to impress us and others by acting grown up, like an adult. Let's show them how to be an adult and not an adulterer.

Dear God, the Holy One, I ask that You help me cleanse my mouth, mind, and heart from all inappropriate sexual thoughts. Give me the strength to stand up to others and refuse to accept or participate in such offenses. Let me teach my children, family, friends, and coworkers not just Your Word, but how much they hurt themselves and others by their actions. Amen.

SEXUAL MATTERS

- Sexual sin adds personal problems to your life and subtracts from your relationship with God.

- You can't hide sin in closets and drawers. You will be exposed. You may not say it out loud, but God can read your mind. He knows your thoughts.

- If you are looking for love in wrong and strange places, you'll never find it because you won't find God in those places and among those people. Nothing goes on behind closed doors that God doesn't see and know.

- It is never too late to make a change; our God is forgiving and gives us the ability to change.

- Don't let your imagination and fantasies put you in a world apart from Christ.

- We are all expected to influence others. Are you influencing others positively or negatively by your actions and words?

- Would you like someone to say to your spouse what you just said to your coworker?

- Would you change your thoughts and words if they were broadcast for all to hear?

- Cleanse your mind on a regular basis.

- Stand up for righteousness among those whose standards have slipped to lowly, lewd levels.

- Obey God in your sexual conduct wherever you are and within any relationship.

- Sexual immorality destroys the very foundation upon which society is built.

- Never forget—the human body is the temple of God. When we degrade His temple with sexual immorality, it's worse than if we spray painted graffiti on a church.

Heavenly Father, there is so much around that tempts me. I pray that I will be strong enough to fight the devil and rely even more on the Holy Spirit You've placed in me, seeking only the joy You can provide. I ask for Your help in guarding my heart, eyes, ears, thoughts, and words. Let my desire be to follow You. Amen.

———————

SCRIPTURE REFERENCES

Proverbs 10:6
Blessings crown the head of the righteous, but violence overwhelms the mouth of the wicked.

Proverbs 13:2-3
From the fruit of his lips a man enjoys good things, but the unfaithful have a craving for violence. He who guards his lips guards his life, but he who speaks rashly will come to ruin.

Psalm 141:3-4
Set a guard over my mouth, O Lord; keep watch over the door of my lips. Let not my heart be drawn to what is evil, to take part in

wicked deeds with men who are evildoers; let
me not eat of their delicacies.

Romans 3:10-14

As it is written: "There is no one righteous, not
even one; there is no one who understands, no
one who seeks God. All have turned away, they
have together become worthless; there is no one
who does good, not even one." "Their throats
are open graves; their tongues practice deceit."
"The poison of vipers is on their lips." "Their
mouths are full of cursing and bitterness."

2 Peter 2:13-14

They will be paid back with harm for the harm
they have done. Their idea of pleasure is to
carouse in broad daylight. They are blots and
blemishes, reveling in their pleasures while
they feast with you. With eyes full of adultery,
they never stop sinning; they seduce the unsta-
ble; they are experts in greed—an accursed
brood!

2 Peter 2:18-22

For they mouth empty, boastful words and, by
appealing to the lustful desires of sinful human
nature, they entice people who are just escaping
from those who live in error. They promise
them freedom, while they themselves are slaves
of depravity—for a man is a slave to whatever

has mastered him. If they have escaped the corruption of the world by knowing our Lord and Savior Jesus Christ and are again entangled in it and overcome, they are worse off at the end than they were at the beginning. It would have been better for them not to have known the way of righteousness, than to have known it and then to turn their backs on the sacred command that was passed on to them. Of them the proverbs are true: "A dog returns to its vomit," and, "A sow that is washed goes back to her wallowing in the mud."

2 Peter 3:17

Therefore, dear friends, since you already know this, be on your guard so that you may not be carried away by the error of lawless men and fall from your secure position.

Hebrews 13:4

Marriage should be honored by all, and the marriage bed kept pure, for God will judge the adulterer and all the sexually immoral.

Ezekiel 23:28-30

For this is what the Sovereign Lord says: I am about to hand you over to those you hate, to those you turned away from in disgust. They will deal with you in hatred and take away everything you have worked for. They will leave you naked and bare, and the shame of your prostitution will be exposed. Your lewdness and promiscuity have brought this upon you, because you lusted after the nations and defiled yourself with their idols.

Ezekiel 23:48-49
So I will put an end to lewdness in the land, that all women may take warning and not imitate you. You will suffer the penalty for your lewdness and bear the consequences of your sins of idolatry. Then you will know that I am the Sovereign Lord.

Ezekiel 24:13
Now your impurity is lewdness. Because I tried to cleanse you but you would not be cleansed from your impurity, you will not be clean again until my wrath against you has subsided.

STEALING

White collar crimes top the news,
    but it's the little crimes that give the company
    the blues.
It's those extra photocopies your daughter was
    needing for those college papers she's reading.
Remember the books you borrow,
    promising to bring them back tomorrow?
What about those extra parking fees you charged as
    expense, all the undocumented dollars and
    cents?
You reached out and touched everyone you could,
    having the company paying what you should.
It was back to school time for the kids,
    so pencils and pens went home, in your brief-
    case well hid.
Now there's talk about cutbacks and severe layoffs,
    the company reports massive losses.
What you gained means nothing now,
    because you contributed to a company falling
    down.
Taking a little here and there seemed harmless,
    now you know the truth since you are jobless.
Don't give in to temptation,
    unless you're prepared to lose your job and
    reputation.

Do not trust in extortion or take pride in stolen goods; though your riches increase, do not set your heart on them.

———————

Sticky Fingers

It is so easy to get into a habit of taking things that don't belong to us, especially in the workplace. We act as if these things belong to us and take advantage of their existence. Many of our employers have made our work environment so comfortable that we sometimes forget that none of these things belong to us.

We don't mean to take things; we may not even realize that we *have* taken something. We get so used to using a particular coffee mug that on the day we left early for a meeting, taking our coffee along with us, we took the mug home and forgot to bring it back. Or after the board meeting, we see that there is leftover food, so we decide to pack up a bag to take home, assuming that no one else had plans for the food and that the food was going to be thrown away. When we order new equipment or supplies, we take home what we had been using. Again, we assume that the company is going to discard it. That may be the case; and if we ask permission, we may very well get to bring home all those extra little things that are no longer needed. On the other hand, when we take a shortcut around asking before we take, we are in effect stealing. And the intent may have been to give the materials to a school or local college or a charity.

Some of us are not so innocent when we purposely take home paper for our computers, sugar packets for our cupboards, napkins for our tables, dictionaries for our children, and more. The company could charge us with petty theft. Worse, God does charge us with committing the sin of stealing—no matter if it is one pencil or a dozen pencils.

Our guilt is just as real when we borrow an item, although we may have gotten permission, and we do not return it because no one asked us for it or seemed to miss it. We sit back and wait for someone to ask for the item to be returned, and until then, we think it's okay to keep it. Guess what? It's not okay, because as long as we have that item, it is considered stolen and God sees us as a thief. He commands us not to steal.

What we have to realize is that breaking into someone's home, robbing a bank, and taking ink pens from the office are all stealing. Each person will be judged regardless of how small the "crime."

Look What I Found: Often we find things on the floor or in the bathroom. We claim these things as ours because we found them; however, if we keep them we have committed an act of stealing. Obviously, the item really doesn't belong to us and someone must have accidentally left it behind. It is our responsibility to try to return the item to its rightful owner. We have plenty of opportunities to do so by first asking if someone lost the item, putting up a note wherever we found the item, seeing if there is a lost-and-found, etc. When we claim a lost item as ours, we are simply claiming the distinction of being a thief.

Morning Prayer

Father in heaven, I give all honor to You, Lord, and pray that I will be honorable in all of my actions. I put on the armor of protection today as I face the temptation to abuse the trust that my employer and coworkers have placed in me. Lord, I don't want to let them down nor do I want to disappoint You. Bind my hands, keeping them free from the sin of stealing. Amen.

TAKE MORE AND GAIN LESS

- The reward for honest, trustworthy actions is always greater than what you would receive otherwise.

- Sin is sin, no matter how big or small. It is committing the "little sins" that can ruin your relationship with God and your ability to set an example for others.

- Regardless of the little things others may do, follow the rules of God which require honesty and result in accountability.

- If you knowingly eat or use something that was stolen, you are just as guilty as the person who stole the item.

- Rejoice in what God has given you instead of desiring what He has given others. If it was meant for you to have it, it would be yours. If you depend totally on God, you won't want for anything because you will have all that you need.

- If you can't tell someone where or how you got something, then it is something you probably should not have in your possession.

- You should not have to hide or conceal what you are taking home. If you have to cover your tracks, you are on the wrong path.

- Stealing shows a lack of faith, patience, and dependence on God.

- You are better off being without than having what you want the wrong way.

- When we steal, we steal from God by not living for Him and not setting a good example for others.

Evening Prayer

God Almighty, I ask for Your guidance in helping me to realize all of the ways that I could steal from You and others. Let me be aware of my past transgressions, forgive me, and keep me from sinning through stealing again. Also, give me the insight and courage to let others around me know of the many ways we steal, especially on the job. Strengthen me to stand for what is right. Amen.

SCRIPTURE REFERENCES

Luke 18:20

You know the commandments: "Do not commit adultery, do not murder, do not steal, do not give false testimony, honor your father and mother."

Leviticus 19:11

Do not steal. Do not lie. Do not deceive one another.

Deuteronomy 5:19

You shall not steal.

Ephesians 4:28

He who has been stealing must steal no longer, but must work, doing something useful with his own hands, that he may have something to share with those in need.

Leviticus 19:13

Do not defraud your neighbor or rob him. Do not hold back the wages of a hired man overnight.

John 10:1

I tell you the truth, the man who does not enter the sheep pen by the gate, but climbs in by some other way, is a thief and a robber.

Isaiah 61:8

For I, the Lord, love justice; I hate robbery and iniquity. In my faithfulness I will reward them and make an everlasting covenant with them.

Ezekiel 18:18

But his father will die for his own sin, because he practiced extortion, robbed his brother and did what was wrong among his people.

Leviticus 6:1-4

The Lord said to Moses: "If anyone sins and is unfaithful to the Lord by deceiving his neighbor about something entrusted to him or left in his care or stolen, or if he cheats him, or if he finds lost property and lies about it, or if he swears falsely, or if he commits any such sin that people may do—when he thus sins and becomes guilty, he must return what he has stolen or taken by extortion, or what was entrusted to him, or the lost property he found."

Habakkuk 2:6-7

Will not all of them taunt him with ridicule and scorn, saying, "Woe to him who piles up stolen goods and makes himself wealthy by extortion! How long must this go on?" Will not your debtors suddenly arise? Will they not wake up and make you tremble? Then you will become their victim.

Luke 12:2

There is nothing concealed that will not be disclosed, or hidden that will not be made known.

CONCLUSION

CONCLUSION

We spend more than half of our time at work. That's one reason why we must make sure that God goes with us to our place of employment. To leave Him out, to compartmentalize this part of our life as something separate from our spiritual life, would be to leave God out of a huge chunk of our time.

God calls us to be whole people, completely committed to Him. That means that He doesn't want us to divide our lives in sections, some pieces influenced by Him and others influenced by the world. Instead, He wants to guide our lives just as much at work as He does when we're at home or church. In fact, we may need His guidance even more during our workday, especially if our workplace is an environment that's not conducive to holiness. Holiness is not an impossible goal; we can rely on Christ's victory in our lives.

As Christians, we should be supporting each other in the workplace, encouraging each other to live up to Christ's standards. What is more, Christ has called us to be light and salt for the world, and our workplace is exactly where He want us to be the most "salty"; after all, it's the dark places that most need the light, and we must remember to let Christ's light shine through us when we're working.

"You're going to have troubles in this world," Jesus said (John 16:33, paraphrased). "But don't be discouraged. I have overcome the world."

Inspirational Library

Beautiful purse/pocket size editions of Christian classics bound in flexible leatherette. These books make thoughtful gifts for everyone on your list, including yourself!

The Bible Promise Book   Over 1000 promises from God's Word arranged by topic. What does God promise about matters like: Anger, Illness, Jealousy, Love, Money, Old Age, and Mercy? Find out in this book!
    Flexible Leatherette $3.97

Daily Light   One of the most popular daily devotionals with readings for both morning and evening.
    Flexible Leatherette $4.97

Wisdom from the Bible   Daily thoughts from Proverbs which communicate truths about ourselves and the world around us.
    Flexible Leatherette $4.97

My Daily Prayer Journal   Each page is dated and features a Scripture verse and ample room for you to record your thoughts, prayers, and praises. One page for each day of the year.
    Flexible Leatherette $4.97

Available wherever books are sold.
Or order from:

Barbour Publishing, Inc.
P.O. Box 719
Uhrichsville, OH 44683
http://www.barbourbooks.com

If you order by mail add $2.00 to your order for shipping.
Prices subject to change without notice.